D1355941

Expert Systems
in Accounting

Expert Systems in Accounting

Alex Edwards

Kingston Business School, Kingston Polytechnic

and

N.A.D. Connell

Department of Accounting and Management Science,
The University of Southampton

Prentice Hall

In association with

The Institute of Chartered Accountants in England and Wales

First published 1989 by
Prentice Hall International (UK) Ltd
66 Wood Lane End, Hemel Hempstead
Hertfordshire, HP2 4RG
A division of
Simon & Schuster International Group

Printed and bound in Great Britain by
BPCC Wheatons Ltd, Exeter.

British Library Cataloguing in Publication Data

Edwards, Alex
  Expert systems in accounting.
  1. Accounting. Applications of expert systems
  I. Title II. Connell, N.A.D.
  657'.028'5633   1636382
  ISBN 0-13-295759-0.

Library of Congress Cataloging-in-Publication Data

Edwards, Alex.
  Expert Systems in accounting / Alex Edwards and N.A.D. Connell.
    p. cm.
  Includes bibliographical references.
  ISBN 0-13-295759-0 : £40.00
  1. Accounting—Data processing. 2. Expert Systems (Computer
science) I. Connell, N.A.D. II. Title.
  HF5679.E24 1990
  657'.0285'633—dc20   89-35890 CIP

1 2 3 4 5 93 92 91 90 89

For

Helen Edwards

and

Linda Connell

Contents

Foreword

The amount of new computing power installed in the world
is doubling every two years. Put another way, the computers
purchased in the next two years will have total processing
power greater than all computers purchased since the beginning of time.

Arthur Andersen & Co.,
Trends in Information Technology (1985)

It is unusual to begin a foreword with a quotation, but the above
illustrates strikingly the current explosive growth in information
technology — or IT as it is more commonly described. One particular
application of the new technology, expert systems, provides enormous
potential for accountants and accounting. The development of expert
systems over the next decade, if successful, is likely to represent one
of the most significant advances in information technology. The
essence of an expert system is its ability to replicate the judgements
and decisions of one or more experts. Such a system could have
dramatic impacts on a variety of accounting functions. For example,
management planning, the choice and application of accounting
methods for external reports (including standard setting), the choice
of sample types and size and the assessment of materiality in auditing, and optimal taxation calculations and planning, are all areas
which require the application of expert judgement. At present, such
decisions involve both the application of routine and well-defined
decision procedures (which can be handled by computer) and the
exercise of judgement (which often can not). A successful expert
system would enable both the routine procedures and the expert
judgements to be undertaken on the computer.

In 1985, recognising the importance of IT developments to
accountants and to industry and commerce generally, the Research
Board of the Institute of Chartered Accountants in England and
Wales set up a two-year senior fellowship in IT which was awarded
to the Department of Accounting and Management Science at the
University of Southampton. Dr Alex Edwards was appointed to the
Fellowship. His brief was to undertake a study of the current role of
expert systems in relation to accounting and to develop an expert

system in the area of the assessment of business risks associated with computer installations. The results of his efforts and of those of several of his colleagues at the University of Southampton, are reported in this book.

The book will be of interest both to the non-specialist reader and to the specialist who is intending to develop an expert system. The non-specialist who wishes to learn more about expert systems will find the first part of the book particularly useful. The authors explain the nature of expert systems, review the current state of affairs in their development and consider their likely future. The material in Part One is supported by three surveys of decision support and expert systems in accounting. Part Two will be of special interest to those who wish to develop their own expert systems. This describes the construction by Dr Edwards of an expert system prototype and lays particular emphasis on the lessons learned in undertaking this project. A real case study of this type often provides many more useful insights than abstract descriptions of hypothetical problems.

IT in general and expert systems in particular will play a crucial role in accounting during the coming years. The Research Board and the Institute of Chartered Accountants in England and Wales are pleased to have been associated with the project reported here. We are indebted to all those who provided assistance and advice, to John Holt and Philip Powell who undertook the survey of decision support systems in accounting, and especially to Alex Edwards and Con Connell who brought the project to fruition.

John Arnold
Director of Research
Institute of Chartered Accountants in England and Wales

Preface

In 1985 the Institute of Chartered Accountants in England and Wales
established a research fellowship in the Department of Accounting
and Management Science of the University of Southampton to investigate the applications of knowledge-based systems in the form of
'expert systems' in accounting and to inform Institute members about
them and how they might be applied in an accounting context.
These objectives were to be achieved through:

(1) a study of the application of expert systems technology in an
    area of interest to the accounting community, the assessment of
    business risks associated with computer installations, including
    (a) the production of a prototype for the above application and
    (b) the generation of commentary regarding the research findings
    and lessons learned during the exercise;
(2) the evaluation and comparison of a number of off-the-shelf
    expert system 'shells' using the implementation of the above
    system as a benchmark;
(3) the completion of a survey on expert systems in accounting,
    concerned with the assessment of the degree to which accounting
    professionals are involved in expert systems developments as well
    as with advances being made in the area by the academic com-
    munity; and
(4) the completion of a survey of decision support systems in ac-
    counting concerned with examining the current state of the
    application of decision support systems for accounting and fi-
    nance functions.

The recipient of the Institute's fellowship, Alex Edwards, undertook
(1) and (2), and collaborated with Con Connell (the Department of
Accounting and Management Science's Arthur Young Fellow) in

addressing (3). Other members of the department, John Holt and Philip Powell, undertook (4).

A number of Institute members made significant contributions. In particular, Arthur Young and Spicer & Oppenheim provided experts for the prototyping exercises. This book summarises the results of the Institute initiative.

Part One of the book provides an introduction to decision support systems and expert systems. Those already familiar with these fields may find it useful to skim read much of this material. The surveys referred to are discussed in detail in the appendices.

Part Two provides an account of that part of the research concerned with the development of the expert system prototype. The style used in this account is often purposely anecdotal. This is in direct response to the general view in the expert systems community that there are too few accounts of exactly what goes on during the difficult process of knowledge elicitation. It is hoped that this account goes some way to addressing that need.

Note. Male personal pronouns have been used throughout this book in order to avoid an over-convoluted style and should not be taken to imply a lack of either female knowledge engineers or female experts, both of which exist in abundance.

Acknowledgements

Kind thanks are due to the following individuals whose contributions were brought to bear through a variety of roles: Professor Andrew Bailey, Mark Bushell, John Court, Mike Dyne, Andrew Gibson, Glen Gray, Professor Bea Helft, Professor Paul Johnson, Professor Ray Meservy, Professor Ted Mock, Professor Ken Nichols, Dan O'Leary, Mike Page, Stuart Turley, Malcom Cooper, Paul Watkins, Professor Clinton White Jr, and Professor Andrew Whinston.

Credit must also be given to the following firms and companies for providing expertise, time, and software: Arthur Andersen, Arthur Young, Binder Hamlyn, Coopers & Lybrand, Deloitte Haskins & Sells, Ernst & Whinney, Grant Thornton, I.S.I., Peat Marwick, SD-Scicon, Spicer and Oppenheim, and Touche Ross.

The survey 'Decision Support Systems in Accounting' was conducted by John Holt and Philip Powell. Our thanks to them for allowing this material to be included in the present work.

We should like to express a word of special appreciation to Professor Chris Chapman who steered and encouraged the work throughout its term, and also to the members of the Department of Accounting and Management Science of Southampton University who supported us in the multitude of ways that happen in a research community.

Finally, thanks are due both to Kingston Business School for making available its excellent desktop publishing facilities for the production of camera-ready copy for this volume and also to Val Jones in her role of production editor for Prentice Hall without whose patience and care the work could not have seen light of day.

Executive Overview

This book evolved out of a research initiative, funded by the Institute of Chartered Accountants in England and Wales (ICAEW), designed to investigate the professional accountant's relationship with decision support software, and in particular with expert systems.

The various elements of the research, developed over a two-year period, are divided between the two parts of the book. Part One (The Research and Development Context) introduces the topic of the book (Chapter 1), discusses the use of decision support systems in an accounting context (Chapter 2) and relates this type of software to expert systems. The reader is then invited to peruse a basic tutorial chapter (Chapter 3) on expert systems before the current state of affairs in expert systems research and development in accounting is reviewed (Chapter 4). This chapter also provides many examples of expert systems which have been implemented in the accounting and finance areas. Finally Chapter 5 looks to the future of expert systems in accounting.

One of the findings in Part One is that despite the general high level of activity in expert systems in some academic departments, expert systems research in accounting is surprisingly limited in scope. Most significant research activity seems to go hand-in glove with what might be called 'early development effort' and is often initiated by the big accounting firms.

During the course of the research three surveys were conducted (the survey reports are reproduced in full in the appendices) The first of these surveys looks at the extent to which accountants are using decision support systems. The second survey reviews the degree to which accountants in both accounting firms and companies are involved in expert system research, construction and use. Finally, the third survey looks in more detail at those organisations that are most heavily involved in this recent technology.

The decision support systems survey (conducted by John Holt and Philip Powell) reveals a surprisingly cautious approach, especially with respect to small firms. This result stands in contrast to the findings of the expert systems surveys which indicate that about half of all respondents are in some way involved in expert systems research and development.

Part Two (A Case Study) reports on the construction of an expert system prototype, developed by the first author. A demonstrator system designed to assess the business risks associated with computer installations was constructed and members of the accounting community were highly cooperative in this venture. This is documented as a case study in full and serves as a reference point for those readers developing their own expert systems and who might wish to gain from the lessons learned in this exercise. Issues such as the difficulties encountered in the knowledge elicitation process and the assessment of potentially viable expert system application areas are addressed. Commentary is also provided regarding what constitutes an appropriate methodology for expert systems construction in a software engineering context. The prototype developed during this phase of the research can be viewed as representing a general architecture for systems that could serve as skills archiving facilities in the area of computer auditing.

PART ONE

The Research and Development Context

In Part One we set out to assess the current level of research and development in expert systems. We explain the technological and commercial environment from which the technology has emerged, showing its roots in mainstream artificial intelligence research and demonstrating how the international competitive climate in the application of this research to commerce has acted as a spur to the development of expert systems. We describe those features of expert systems which distinguish them from similar technologies such as decision support systems, and stress the significance of expertise as an ingredient in such systems. We show that the role of the user is critical in the design and construction of successful systems. We examine the various applicatons of expert systems and highlight those aspects of the technology that might make it of particular interest to the accounting profession. Finally, we look at the possible effects on the profession of the implementation of such systems by examining the impact they might have on a firm's internal operations and on its relationship with its clients and with its competitors.

Chapter 1

Introduction

Last year I couldn't even spell knowledge engineer, now I R1.
(after McDermott 1982)

1.1 What is an Expert System?

There is no widely accepted definition of an expert system. The
term itself is shrouded in confusion, sometimes being used synony-
mously with knowledge-based system, intelligent knowledge-based
system, artificial intelligence (AI) system, decision support system,
management support system, smart system, or intelligent system.
These distinctions are discussed in more detail in Chapter 3, where
we offer examples of definitions, and compare functional and architectural definitions. For the purposes of this introductory chapter,
let us bypass this debate by compromising a little, and defining an
expert system as follows:

> a computer-based system in which representations of exper-
> tise are stored and which allows a user to access this exper-
> tise in a way similar to that in which he might consult a
> human expert, with a similar result.

Such a definition begs a number of questions. How is the expertise
stored? How can the system be interrogated? How can the user be
sure that the system has considered all the possibilities? How can
the user be certain that the system is providing the right advice at
the end of the consultation? The answer to most of these questions
is the same as would be expected if one were asking them of a
human expert — either we don't know or we can't be certain. With
a human expert we sometimes ask for an explanation of how he or
she reached a conclusion. We may also wish to alter the parameters
of the problem, to see if such modification affects the decision. And
we may of course choose to ignore the expert's advice completely.

One thing is clear; for a computer system to be classed as an expert system, it must somehow embody a representation of expertise. Consequently the treatment of expertise runs as a fundamental thread throughout this book. It is the nature of expertise, its relationship with data and knowledge, and its role in the decision-making process, that forms the basis of Chapter 2. Chapter 3 provides basic material about the nature of expert systems. Chapter 4 surveys those areas of an accountant's expertise that have already been investigated in both the UK and USA for their applicability as expert systems, and charts the progress already made in this area by a number of accounting firms and academic researchers, but still with the focus very much on the nature of that expertise which lends itself to development. Chapter 5 demonstrates that technological considerations are unlikely to prove the only constraint to the wider development of expert systems, by concluding that expertise has an important contextual dimension that cannot be ignored.

The remainder of this introductory chapter is concerned with setting the scene by reminding the reader of the information technology (IT) environment of the mid-1980s when this work was initiated, and recognising how the accounting profession interacted within this environment.

1.2 Commercial Expert Systems Development in the Early 1980s

Case histories of users who have derived great financial benefit from the introduction of expert systems are not common, and were less so in the mid-1980s. Working expert systems do exist; some are even successful such as, the much publicised systems which assist in the configuration of computer installations (e.g. XCON (McDermott 1982), DRAGON (Keen 1983) and similar systems used by IBM and Nixdorf). Yet these and other successful systems operate in technical domains, rather than in the domains of main-stream business management or commerce. One of the reasons for this non-commercial emphasis in the development of the early expert systems is due to the nature of the expertise within these domains; the ease with which expertise can be captured and made usable by a computer system will contribute greatly to the success of that system and some application areas intrinsically lend themselves better to expert system application than others (for an explanation of why this might be so, see the discussion of domain selection in Chapter 3). The second reason for the industrial/technical, rather than commercial, emphasis of the pioneering application domains was probably because expert systems had arisen initially out of the work carried out by the AI community, which was traditionally involved with more technically oriented domains. The historical reasons for this are briefly discussed in the following section.

1.3 Artificial Intelligence and Expert System Applications

AI research has a long history across a broad spectrum of disciplines. *The Handbook of Artificial Intelligence* (Barr and Feigenbaum 1981) lists some of the aspects of intelligent behaviour that AI researchers are addressing, including problem solving, logical reasoning, language manipulation, learning, robotics and vision, and expertise. Not all their efforts have been well received, even by the research community; the evaluation of AI's contribution to scientific research, as expressed in the infamous Lighthill Report, declared the work 'sadly wanting at best and bordering on charlatanism at worst' (Feigenbaum and McCorduck 1983). However, by the early 1980s the thrust of much of AI's early *practical* application was in the direction of robotics, particularly industrial robotics. It is therefore to be expected that where collaborative ventures were to be undertaken between teams of researchers and industrialists, those with an experience of working successfully together in the development of computer-based systems to manipulate physical objects might feel equally comfortable working towards the development of computer-based systems to manipulate mental, rather than physical, processes.

1.4 The Impact of the Japanese Fifth-Generation Project

At the beginning of the 1980s, there was a further need to reappraise the role intelligent computer systems might play in the coming decade. The Japanese Ministry of International Trade and Industry announced their ambitious ten-year plan to develop the next generation of computer systems. This 'fifth' generation would have at its heart knowledge-based systems. In 1982 the first stage in the ten-year programme was marked by the establishment of the Institute for New Generation Computer Technology (ICOT). A key element of the development programme was to be the close cooperation between academics and industrialists.

The UK response to the Japanese initiative was the announcement, in 1982, of its own initiative. The Alvey Committee outlined plans for a five-year programme of government-supported collaboration between academe and industry under four broad research areas: software engineering (SE), very-large-scale integration (VLSI), the man–machine interface (MMI) and intelligent knowledge based systems (IKBS). In addition to large 'demonstrator' projects, some smaller projects would be funded and a number of community clubs would be set up under the auspices of the Alvey committee to further research and development in specific areas of interest to, and determined by, club members. A number of the larger accounting firms took an active role in these clubs, particularly in Alfex (Alvey Financial Expert systems) and Aries (Alvey Research into Insurance Expert Systems).

A typical outcome of the clubs' activities was the construction of prototype expert systems; for example, the Alfex Club members agreed jointly to construct a company financial health adviser within the specific domain (for the pilot project) of high-technology retailing. A financial consultant could use such a system to assess the long-term viability of the retailer under examination and thus form a more 'expert' opinion of risks relating to loanworthiness. The prototype system offered advice as the consultation developed and at the end of the consultation gave advice in the form of sales projection figures, an opinion on the reasonableness of management projections with which it had been provided, and advice on 'company sensitivities', indicating those variables which are likely to prove critical for this company's future.

In common with most other Alvey clubs, membership was drawn from competitors in the chosen field; in the case of the Alfex club members were from the larger banks and accounting firms. The focus of interest of the clubs' membership was not confined to the systems built, but also to the lessons learned during the construction process. Perhaps it is hardly surprising, therefore, that many of the accounting firms who participated were represented by the management consultancy divisions of their organisations who might benefit from passing these lessons on to clients.

1.5   The Growth in the Expert Systems Market

The worldwide activity in expert systems fuelled by such government funding and stimulated by articles and books such as *The Fifth Generation* (Feigenbaum and McCorduck 1983) led to a flurry of activity in expert systems. The mid-1980s is already being looked back upon as the great period of expert system 'hype', evidenced by projected sales of 'intelligent' products or their derivatives which were estimated to be between $100 million (Friscia 1985) and $300 million (Frost and Sullivan 1985). Figures for the expert system element of this total varied; *MIS Week* in January 1985 stated that 'Today's $20 million expert system market should reach $2.5 billion by 1993'.

The Ovum Report (Hewett and Sasson 1986) put sales of expert systems at $70 million in 1985, a figure confirmed by Livingstone, writing in *High Technology* (1986), who expected this figure to double ($140 million) in 1986, with a projected $810 million by 1990. Earlier in 1986, *Fortune* magazine had stated that 'Sales of expert systems reached $216 million [in 1985]. Industry analysts project a $3.5 billion market by 1990.' Whatever the precise figures, the mid-1980s appeared to be a turning point for expert systems. Organisations were showing a willingness to spend money investigating the subject and some areas were seeing a clear movement from research to application.

The range of applications in the mid-1980s was wide but with a firm emphasis on problem domains which were well structured. A review of working expert systems carried out at about this time (Buchanan 1986) listed about sixty systems which had progressed beyond the development laboratories into field test or live environments. The systems were classified within twelve broad application domains, such as agriculture, medicine, etc. Not surprisingly, the computer and electronics sub-domain had the most applications (twenty-two) followed by manufacturing and engineering (fourteen). Of those areas that might typically be thought of as relating closely to accountancy, only three systems were cited in the financial sub-domain, and only one in what the review described as 'information management'. Financial systems, heralded as an area particularly suited to the application of expert systems (Clarke and Cooper 1985; McReynolds 1984), seem to have had a low profile. The financial community was either doing very little, or keeping very quiet about what it was doing. If expert system activity was beginning to blossom in some domains, it did not appear that accountancy was one of them. It was upon this possibility that the Institute's programme of research sought to focus.

1.6   The Accountant and Expert Systems

If the initial response of the accounting profession to the new technology did not appear to match the flurry of activity in the exploitation of commercial expert systems that appeared to be taking place
in some sectors of the computing, engineering and manufacturing
industries, it was not because accountants as a body had an aversion
to the use of IT as a part of their everyday operations. The large
professional accounting firms, and many of the smaller practices,
have recognised the value of computer systems to their internal
operations. The development of expertise in the handling of such
systems, borne partly of a need to become familiar with the systems
of clients, has enabled the larger accounting firms to be well placed
to embrace any new developments in computing. Perhaps due to the
decentralised nature of their operations, accounting firms have expressed great interest in distributed/decentralised computing systems,
of which the microcomputer is the primary example. Researchers
who had undertaken detailed examinations of the way in which, by
the mid-1980s, accountants were using IT systems, provide ample
evidence of the range and depth of this use. Collier (1984) surveyed
400 members of the Institute of Cost and Management Accountants
working in the UK private sector. He concluded that their involvement in the development and use of computer systems was widespread, and singled out decision support systems as 'playing an
increasingly important role in the work of many accountants'. Expert
systems, although mentioned, were labelled very much as a 'future
development'.

The survey undertaken the following year by Clarke and
Cooper (1985) saw the likely potential of expert systems assuming a
significantly higher profile. Respondents were asked to identify the
IT developments they believed would be commonplace in the next
two, five or ten years. Cumulative percentages were as follows:

		Industry and Commerce			Accountancy Firms		
Expert systems for	years	2	5	10	2	5	10
tax, audit and other							
accounting areas	%	17	55	84	12	57	83

Clarke and Cooper comment that these responses indicate that expert
systems were identified as one of the four development areas most

likely to become commonplace in the following ten years, the others being the use of external databases, individual workstations for professional staff, and computer-assisted learning. Of expert systems, they felt it was difficult to gauge the potential impact, although they identified two probable roles for such systems.

First, the assistance in complex tasks for less skilled practitioners. They added the caveat that although such applications might be limited in their capabilities, they would be sufficiently powerful to need to remain under the control of the professional accountant, to avoid the danger of 'other groups of financial advisers (exploiting) this service to the client' (Clarke and Cooper 1985, Section 320).

Second, an important role for expert systems was envisaged as a tool for the prediction of organisational performance from financial ratios. It was claimed that such a use could prove beneficial to financial analysts, auditors and the company itself.

1.7 Conclusions

The accounting profession certainly has a finger firmly upon the IT pulse and has been aware of, and in some instances involved in, the early development of expert systems in commercial environments in the UK. It might therefore seem reasonable to expect that the profession would be quick to appreciate the benefits of expert systems and to be implementing systems without delay. One way in which such an hypothesis might be tested would be to assess the use to which decision support systems had been put and to assess whether the profession felt, as Clarke and Cooper seem to suggest, that expert systems merited singling out for special attention. The following chapter explores this hypothesis in greater depth, examining in particular the relationship between expert systems and decision support systems (DSS).

Chapter 2

Decision Support Systems in Accounting

2.1 The Decision Support Function

One of the principal motivations behind the work reported in this book arose out of the ICAEW's concern with the nature of decision making, and the ways in which computer-based systems can assist in, or even replicate, the decision-making processes. The psychological and organisational foundations underpinning this fascinating yet complex subject are not examined in detail here; readers are referred to Newell and Simon (1980) and Hogarth (1987). We are here concerned with decision making in an accounting context: how might the practising accountant bring his or her expertise to bear when confronted with a situation that requires the application of judgement? And how might a computer-based system, which we traditionally think of as being most usefully applied in situations which are repetitive or deterministic rather than judgemental, be constructed in such a way as to assist an accountant lacking in that expertise?

Our orientation in this chapter is therefore a functional one; we see decision making as the balancing of evidence for or against a particular course of action and the employment of tools, particularly computer-based tools, that assist in this process. Although the expert system has been the tool at the centre of our research efforts, we cannot ignore other computer systems that aid decision making, such as decision support systems and management support systems, particularly because the distinctions between such systems and expert systems are not clear-cut.

Some readers may find this need for distinction unnecessary. If a system performs a given task adequately, then what does it matter whether we call it an expert system or decision support system? The distinction is merited for two reasons.

First, if expert systems are merely another form of decision support system, then their introduction within most accounting firms ought to be smooth and rapid. There is a significant body of knowledge, both in research and development, in decision support systems and their application. Most of the larger firms have decision support systems expertise, and it might be reasonable to expect that decision support systems managers would anticipate little difficulty in finding applications for expert systems. However, this view is not borne out by the survey responses (see Appendix A). Decision support systems managers see sufficient distinction between expert systems and decision support systems to be able to make assertions about their comparative use within their firms and have a clear view of the role of each. If, as we contend, expert systems are different by virtue of their focus upon knowledge rather than data, then it is to be expected that their scope of application will be different and they will need to be developed in different ways from decision support systems. The survey responses are consistent with this view. This chapter examines the implications of these differences.

Second, the understandable desire of most accounting firms to be seen by their clients and competitors to be abreast of the latest developments in IT may have contributed to the need for a clear distinction, in terms of functionality at least, between decision support systems and expert systems. We need to establish that this difference is more than purely cosmetic.

There is more to this line of argument than just 'sociological semantics' (Schwartz 1977). The possibility of fiercely competitive financial exploitation of 'state of the art' ideas in IT may lead to an obfuscation of any debate on the differences between decision support systems and expert systems. There may be more money to be made from marketing a piece of software as an expert system than as a decision support system, irrespective of its architecture or functionality. This chapter focuses upon the commercial significance of such differences, particularly the way in which these differences affect how decision support systems and expert systems may be developed.

In the following section we begin by examining the characteristics of data and knowledge. We then consider whether these characteristics assist in distinguishing between decision support systems and expert systems, and examine some of the distinctions between the two types of system made by other researchers. Finally, we consider the different ways in which these systems contribute to the decision support function.

2.2   Data and Knowledge

Although it is not our purpose to delve too deeply into the semantics surrounding the distinctions between data and knowledge, we must begin by recognising a distinction between data-based and knowledge-based systems. One view might be that the raw materials of each of these systems falls into two broad classes, numeric and symbolic, and that the decision support tools that are best suited for dealing with these two types of evidence are decision support systems and expert systems, respectively. Thus, if numbers are interpreted as data and symbols as knowledge, then it may be said that whereas a decision support systems operates through the manipulation of data, an expert system operates through the manipulation of knowledge. However, this distinction between decision support systems and expert systems, whilst convenient, is not one that finds universal support in the decision support research literature, where, although it is generally recognised that the roots of expert systems are in artificial intelligence, their place among the branches of problem-solving methodology does not seem so clear. Some commentators have argued that expert systems do not differ to any great degree from traditional problem-oriented software (Martins 1984), others that they are an interesting variation upon the already well documented field of decision support systems (Ford 1985; Holsapple and Whinston 1985; Sen and Biswas 1985). Others have argued that the use of such systems in management application merits an alternative title, management support systems (MSS) (Lee 1983; Blanning 1984).

The Institute was mindful of some of these distinctions at the inception of the research programme, and therefore supported the funding of two parallel surveys, each focusing on a different aspect of computer-based decision support.

The remainder of this chapter examines in more detail these distinctions and assesses their significance for the tasks of the accountant.

2.3   Distinguishing between Decision Support Systems and Expert Systems

Stoner (1984), commenting on the likely application of expert systems to the accounting profession, proposed placing expert systems and decision support systems along a continuum of management tools, their position on the continuum being determined by their complexity. There are drawbacks in the use of complexity (by which we mean structural or architectural complexity rather than environmental complexity) as a discriminatory device, since this criterion seems to exclude the possibility of building a simple (that is, non-complex) expert system. However, Stoner admits to a fuzzy region in which it is difficult to draw a boundary between such systems, suggesting that the ability of an expert system to 'apply and justify judgement' distinguishes it from a decision support system. He further argues that because the role of an accountant involves the communication of economic events to individuals, an ability to interact with the system in some sort of 'natural language' is invaluable.

Other comparisons in the literature have concentrated on the architectural differences between decision support systems and expert system.

For expert systems, the architectural principles emerged from empirical observation of early construction efforts (Davis 1982). The accepted view is that an expert system must include as prerequisites a knowledge base, an inference engine and a user interface. A knowledge acquisition system and explanation facilities are often explicit subsystems, yet are sometimes implicit; see, for example, the model in Harmon and King (1985). Other definitions have a more functional orientation, broadly along the lines that the system must in some way model the behaviour of a domain expert.

For decision support systems, the architectural principles seem equally clear. The generic architectural framework suggested by Bonczek *et al.* (1980) has a 'generality, simplicity and capability for extensive elaboration' (Holsapple and Whinston 1985). The framework incorporates three elements, a language system, a problem processing system, and a knowledge system. Of a decision support system's knowledge system Holsapple and Whinston (1985) state:

> A decision support systems must possess application-specific knowledge about the   decision making system's problem domain.

Comparing this decision support system model with the expert system model outlined above, the areas of overlap become clear, and arguments that it ought to be possible to distinguish between decision support systems and expert systems on the grounds that the latter is knowledge-based, whilst the former is data-based, seem less firmly grounded. Using Bonczek's criteria, expert systems should be considered a subset of decision support systems. The situation is not eased by the introduction of the third essential ingredient in both decision support systems and expert system, expertise, which might loosely be equated to Holsapple and Whinston's reasoning or meta-knowledge.

Holsapple and Whinston (1985) distinguish between the *process* of decision making and the *content*. A process orientation focuses upon the stages through which decision making passes, whereas a content orientation is more concerned with the individual decision maker and the outcome of the decision. They conclude that an examination of process frameworks such as that suggested by Simon (1960) assist a decision support systems builder in differentiating between well-structured and ill-structured problems, but have less to offer in the construction of the system itself, be it decision support system or expert system. They therefore concentrate on content frameworks, an examination of which might lead to a fuller understanding of the decision-making process and the characteristics required of a decision support system. They identify seven 'abilities' required of a decision support systems: information collection, formulation, governing, analysis, evaluation, problem recognition, and implementation. They suggest that these abilities will be shared between the user and the decision support systems, and that abilities may be configured in different ways. The configuration of these abilities can then be used as a mechanism for comparing internal structures and therefore, as noted earlier, the primary focus is architectural in the sense of providing an appropriate foundation upon which the decision support system may be built. Within this content-oriented approach, they suggest these abilities interact within the generic architectural framework referred to above, comprising a language system, a knowledge system and a problem-processing system. Let us examine each element of this architectural framework in more depth.

2.3.1 The language system

The language system provides the means by which the user can enter data or define parameters. Much has been written on this user interface, in both the decision support system and the expert system literature. Within the field of AI there is a long tradition of researching and designing languages that are equally intelligible to machine and man, and much of this work can be applied to decision support systems. For an interesting and readable introduction to this area, the reader is referred to Boden (1977) Chapters 5–7.

2.3.2 The knowledge system

A decision support system must contain information about the problem domain. We have seen above that defining knowledge, or even differentiating between data and knowledge, is not always a straightforward task. Holsapple and Whinston suggest that at there are at least seven distinct kinds of application-specific knowledge:

Empirical or environmental knowledge, which is that drawn by observation or other means from the problem domain.

Modelling knowledge, which might take the form of computations which need to be performed to derive new knowledge from empirical knowledge.

Derived knowledge, the product of this computation.

Reasoning, sometimes called meta-knowledge, the knowledge about how knowledge might be applied; this type of knowledge most closely resembles the 'expertise' embodied within an expert system.

Assimilative knowledge, the knowledge of learning and of knowing what new knowledge needs to be retained.

Linguistic knowledge, a knowledge of the rules of language that will govern the operation of the language system referred to above.

Presentation knowledge, a knowledge of how interaction with the user might best be controlled, implicit within which is a knowledge of the user.

2.3.3 The problem-processing system

The problem-processing system is the kernel of the decision support systems. It receives input from the user via the language system and draws upon knowledge resident in its knowledge system. These inputs are then processed, perhaps according to the 'abilities' which the system possesses, and the results presented to the user.

Thus it is argued that the issue of distinguishing between decision support systems and expert systems is resolved by applying the criteria provided by the generic decision support system framework (that is, the possession of a language system, knowledge system and problem-processing system). Holsapple and Whinston, in claiming that expert systems fall within such a framework, conclude that the lessons learned by decision support systems builders are no less pertinent to the construction of expert systems.

2.4   Functional Differences between Decision Support Systems and Expert Systems

From the above we see that reference to architectural differences to distinguish between decision support systems and expert systems seems far from straightforward. A contrasting approach is to compare their functionality, describing the features of each. The most comprehensive comparison is that of Turban and Watkins (1988), who suggest eleven attributes that may be used to contrast decision support systems and expert systems. These attributes centre around the nature of the problem (its uniqueness and complexity), the deciding agent (whether human or machine), the nature of the support given by the system (its reasoning characteristics and explanation capability, the direction of dialogue initiation), and the nature of the system itself (its objectives and function, its method of knowledge manipulation).

A classification approach which takes a functional perspective is that proposed by Connell and Powell (1987). It acknowledges architectural differences but does not focus upon them. It compares the decision maker's contribution to the decision process with the contribution made by the system, and uses this balance as a means of classifying the system. This emphasis on the extent of user input to the decision process is termed the value-added model. This approach is similar to that of Ford (1985), who uses four criteria to compare decision support systems and expert systems, one of which is the user of the system. However, Ford concentrates on the different class of user who will be attracted to decision support system or expert system use, suggesting the former will attract the 'business' user whilst the latter will attract the 'research' user. Ford further suggests that the expertise to be modelled will be high-level, and that those engaged in the use of the system will not have had a hand in its development. This statement may have become the victim of the passage of time. Certainly it is not entirely borne out by either the current research activity nor the findings of the questionnaires (see Chapter 4 and Appendices A and B). However, it is clear that if the use of the system is to be at the management rather than technical level, the development of MSS merits separate investigation.

2.5 Management Support Systems

When we are talking of management in the context of the accounting profession, what precisely do we mean? Mintzberg's (1973) empirical study of managerial activities suggested that the overwhelming majority of management time was spent in some form of interaction with others, either communicating or gathering data about the operational environment for which he or she was responsible. Lee (1983) suggests that this pattern of activity demonstrates that managerial expertise is inevitably organisational:

> rather than possessing an individual expertise, [managers] are more like specialised nodes in a larger 'organisational cognition'.

In this sense, the management support system can only assist and augment this human cognition, never replace it. How can this assistance be brought about in an accounting context? And are the management tasks within the profession any different from those that a manager of a manufacturing plant or a general hospital might face? Consider, as an example, one facet of the accountant's work, the typical annual audit performed by an accounting firm. It could be argued that there is no such thing as a typical audit. However, if we consider the procedures listed in the Institute's Auditing Standards and Guidelines (ICAEW 1980), we can see that certain tasks are necessary in order to fulfil the audit function. How is management expertise employed in this function? How might an expert system assist?

For the purposes of our example, consider a simplified management structure comprising three tiers: junior staff who may not be fully qualified, seniors, and partners. For the larger accounting firms, most of the day-to-day aspects of the audit will be handled by junior staff. Often their task is made easier by the use of 'audit programmes', perhaps taking the form of a checklist of questions and activities. Junior staff will be expected to manage, in the sense of apportioning time and resources sensibly, but the nature of that management is essentially self-management at the operational level. On a larger audit, with a number of junior staff involved, the smooth conduct of the audit will require the 'senior' acting as the operational manager, ensuring that the correct tasks are performed within the required parameters. It is unlikely that the senior management of the firm, a partner for example, would need to intervene other than on an exception basis.

This rather crude characterisation of the respective roles of management staff is not meant to do any more than highlight the notion that, irrespective of the nature of the organisation, the key task of the manager is to monitor and control. What makes it difficult for computer systems to undertake similar activities with equal success is the unstructured nature of management (Gorry and Scott-Morton 1971, Keen and Scott-Morton 1978). The further up the traditional management hierarchy one travels, the more unstructured are the tasks. The distance necessary to travel up the hierarchy before this lack of structure becomes a prevailing feature of the decision process differs for different organisations. Because of the operational environment, we might expect to encounter it at a lower level in a general hospital than in a manufacturing enterprise, for example. In an accounting firm it could be expected at a very low level in the hierarchy.

Expert systems operate best in well structured domains. Does this mean that expert systems cannot provide support for management tasks? Blanning (1984) indicates that some work has been attempted in three sub-categories of the monitor and control functions:

Resource allocation, particularly the allocation of financial resources such as research and development budgets to particular projects, but also the allocation of financial resources to particular investments.

Problem diagnosis, to help identify and correct situations that are susceptible to corporate ill health in the same way that a physician might look for indicators of physical ill health.

Scheduling and assignment, particularly the allocation of scarce resources or the assignment of individuals to tasks.

One could find applications in the simplified auditing example mentioned above for all three of these sub-categories. In fact, Blanning uses an audit application (Dungan 1983, and described in Chapter 4) as an illustration of how such systems might be implemented.

2.6   The Decision Support Function: Conclusions

In this chapter we have highlighted some of the difficulties encountered in attempting to distinguish between decision support systems and expert systems. We have indicated that it is possible to compare such systems architecturally and functionally. Architecturally it appears difficult to differentiate them for two reasons.

The first is the lack of a precise distinction between data-based and knowledge-based systems. If knowledge is taken as being domain-specific data, and we are dealing with domains which are inherently ill-structured and ill-bounded, then in some circumstances definitions such as Bonczek's will lead us toward the conclusion that almost all data is knowledge, and every database a knowledge base. Such definitions are reminiscent of the problems encountered by the AI community in trying to define intelligence; it was often their plaintive cry that as soon as they had constructed a piece of software capable of performing an 'intelligent' task, critics would argue that such a task could not possibly be construed as intelligent since it could be performed by a computer! The same arguments apply to expertise and are exacerbated by the wide-ranging definitions of decision support systems to be found in the research literature.

The second reason is that definitions run the risk of falling foul of the 'criterial properties' problem noted by Lee (1983): the set of properties that a system must possess will either be so broad that too many things qualify, or so restrictive that atypical systems will be excluded.

Turning to functional distinctions between expert systems and decision support systems, we have demonstrated that their commonality lies in the extent to which they contribute to the decision process. This contribution may be determined by the organisational level at which the decision is to be made, which is perhaps a function of the existing expertise of the user or the size of the potential user population within any one organisation. We have also noted that management decisions are characterised by their lack of structure and that computer-based decision support tools can be of only limited assistance in such circumstances. The assistance offered by expert systems is the provision of expertise. It is the treatment of expertise, particularly the way in which this expertise is available to the user, which is the key difference between expert systems and decision support systems. This feature, more than any other, characterises expert systems and should serve as a pointer to the importance of the user in the expert system development methodology. This is not to deny that user considerations are important in decision support systems development. In expert systems, however, the user will determine not only the way in which expertise is recalled during the system's operation, but also the level of expertise. Such demands require a different approach to the development of expert systems than decision support systems.

This study therefore made a distinction between decision support systems and expert systems which was functional rather than architectural, and undertook extensive surveys of both types of system. The results of these surveys are reproduced in detail in Appendices A, B and C. The reader is referred to Appendix A for a discussion of the use made of decision support systems by the accounting profession. It was clear that the respondents to the decision support systems survey had little difficulty in distinguishing between the two types of system but that their experiences with decision support systems had not encouraged them to the view that they ought to ensure a place for expert systems in their firm's IT plans. On the contrary, the decision support systems survey suggests a bleak outlook for expert systems. Whilst this was not entirely reflected by the results arising from the expert systems surveys, it does suggest that the impetus for expert systems development will not be restricted to those accountants responsible for decision support systems development in the firm. In view of the user orientation referred to above, it is hardly surprising that developments in other commercial and industrial sectors have often been initiated by those outside the specialist information systems field, and it is to be expected that the same development pattern will be true in the accounting profession. In many of the prototype accounting systems described in Chapter 4, the developer or joint developer has been a functional specialist rather than an IT system developer.

In this chapter we have demonstrated that the difference between decision support systems and expert systems is not trivial, nor is it merely semantics. If the functional and architectural aspects of expert systems are to be exploited commercially, a new methodology is demanded which pays the closest attention to user considerations. Such a methodology is discussed in Part Two. In the following chapter we describe in more detail the functional and architectural aspects of expert systems and examine some non-accounting applications where they have been used to advantage.

Chapter 3

Background to Expert Systems

This chapter provides an introduction to the main technical concepts associated with the structure of an expert system. It begins with a short discussion of the debate surrounding the definition of what an expert system is. It then describes in overview the functional constituents of an expert system, recalls a widely used classification for expert system tasks, and provides some examples of actual systems. The chapter continues with a review of the benefits which are generally thought should accrue from the use of expert systems and then considers reasons for the apparent dearth of operating systems. Finally, brief mention is made of the kind of tools which are used to construct expert systems.

3.1   Definitions

Opinions as to what exactly systems are tend to fall into one of two camps:

Definition 1 (BCS, Expert Systems Specialist Group)
'An expert system is a computer system containing an organised body of knowledge which emulates expert problem solving skills in a bounded domain of expertise. The system is able to achieve expert levels of problem solving performance which would normally be achieved by a skilled human when confronted with significant problems in the domain.'

Definition 2 (Goodall 1985)
'An expert system is a computer system that operates by applying an inference mechanism to a body of specialist expertise represented in the form of "knowledge".'

The first definition contains both *process*-oriented and *outcome*-oriented elements. It prescribes (indirectly) both how an expert system comes to its judgements ('. . . emulates expert solving skills . . .') and also the desired level of performance ('. . . able to achieve expert levels of . . .'). The second definition is based upon how the system is constructed, its *architecture*. These two approaches may be referred to as representing respectively the 'functionalist' and 'architecturalist' points of view.

There is another point of view, which maintains that semantic hair-splitting is a waste of time, and that so long as a piece of software is useful it doesn't really matter what one chooses to call it. The principal debate, however, lies between the protagonists of function and the champions of architecture.

From a functional perspective, an expert system may be said to be a computer system which exhibits or mimics the cognitive behaviour of a human expert. The characteristics of human expert behaviour, in the context of a consultation with an enquirer, include the ability to reason through the manipulation of concepts and rules-of-thumb acquired over many years of experience; the ability to cope with uncertain or incomplete evidence; the ability to explain the need for more information; the ability to justify conclusions; the ability to negotiate, through knowledge of the enquirer, the most appropriate content level for the consultation, and the ability to satisfy a variety of lines of enquiry during the course of a dialogue. Furthermore, an expert is able easily to maintain his store of knowledge and keep it up to date. A functionalist would argue that such 'ease of maintenance' should also be true of an expert system.

An appreciation of the architectural viewpoint, requires some historical perspective. Expert systems have arisen as a development within the more general discipline of AI, which has been an area of academic research for some thirty years. A central idea in AI is the manipulation of symbols, which can represent ideas, concepts, and so on. The key to knowledge-based systems lies in their use of symbol manipulation. Concepts and hypotheses, which are the everyday fare of the human expert, are represented by symbols and are dealt with in a very direct way. The AI community developed tools and techniques to aid them in this 'symbol manipulation', and these techniques were used in the development of the first expert systems. Hence, views on what are the most appropriate architectures for expert systems have evolved from associated AI research. 'Appropriate' here generally means that the inference and control functions of the system are separated out from the part which contains the knowledge. These two aspects of an expert system are referred to as the inference engine and the knowledge base, respectively. In addition, the system must communicate with its user and this is achieved through a so-called user interface.

There are more complex variations on this theme, but the lines of functional demarcation are clear. Those who subscribe to the architectural view say that a system is an expert one by virtue of its having an inference engine separated from a knowledge base upon which it operates, the latter constituting 'data' for the former, the two being linked to the user via a user interface.

But the debate does not end here. Among the functionalists there are those who maintain the view that an expert system should be primarily outcome-oriented, the emphasis being on its high-performance problem-solving ability. Others maintain that the important criterion is the degree to which the reasoning processes traced by a system in solving a problem are the same as those experienced by a human expert in solving the same problem. In this case outcome is relatively unimportant but what is crucial is the fidelity of the model to the intermediate human cognitive processes.

3.2 Anatomy

As discussed above, expert systems are generally considered to have three essential components — a knowledge base, an inference engine, and a user interface (see Figure 3.1).

3.2.1 The knowledge base

The power of an expert system lies in its knowledge base, an ensemble of structures that represent, in a clear way, the knowledge elicited from an expert.

The particular form that these structures take is related to the way in which the knowledge is perceived to be best represented and manipulated. Paradigms for the representation of knowledge include production rules, semantic nets and frames.

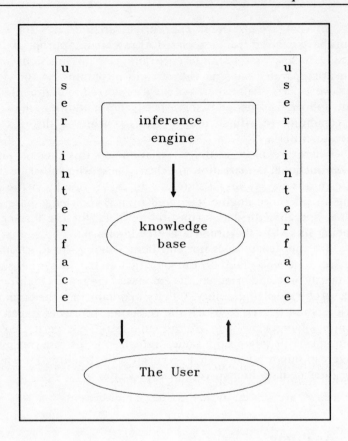

Figure 3.1 The structure of an expert system.

Production rules

A production rule is a structure which has the form:

IF <antecedents> THEN <consequent>

The antecedents in this formalism represent the set of conditions which are sufficient for the establishment of the consequent. In general the consequent may be some assertion or it may be an injunction to perform some action.

Here is an example of a production rule taken from the model described in Part Two of this book:

IF	sign-on security is used
AND	menu security is used
AND	resource security is used
THEN	overall controls are good

In this example the concepts 'sign-on security is used', 'menu security is used', 'resource security is used' and 'overall controls are good' are represented in the computer (i.e. in the knowledge base) by tokens or symbols that are manipulated according to the laws of logic by the control procedures which are effected by the inference engine. It is easy to appreciate that a knowledge base containing hundreds of such production rules might well exhibit fairly complex reasoning behaviour when under the operation of the inference engine.

The use of production rules can boast of several advantages (Barr and Feigenbaum 1981). They exhibit *modularity* in as much as they behave as chunks of knowledge which are operationally independent of one another. The knowledge expressed by production rules has a *uniform* structure imposed on it by the IF . . . THEN . . . framework. This serves to make the knowledge more easily understood by other people. Also, the mode of expression used in production rules may be considered *natural* in as much as it corresponds directly with how a human would express his or her knowledge. On the other hand, production systems (as collections of production rules are termed) are generally *inefficient* in implementation this being directly due to the overhead incurred through their inherent modular and uniform structure. Production systems also exhibit *opacity* since it is often difficult to follow the flow of control in a system during problem-solving. To date, however, production systems are the most widely used method of representing knowledge.

Semantic nets
A semantic net is a network which consists of nodes interconnected by links. The nodes represent objects ('man', 'woman', 'George') and the interconnecting links represent relationships ('is_a', 'has_profession'). A simple example of such a net is shown in Figure 3.2. This net expresses the facts that a woman (WOMAN_1 who is a member of the set of WOMEN) called ETHEL is married to a man (MAN_1 who is a member of the set of MEN) called GEORGE who is an ACCOUNTANT. The 'is_a' link is known as the 'property inheritance link'. This kind of link may be used to infer facts which are not expressed explicitly in the net. For example, it may be deduced that George is a PRIMATE since George is identified with the particular MAN_1 and therefore inherits all of the general

properties of this object. Likewise MAN_1 inherits all of the general properties of MAN, which inherits its properties from the set PRI-MATE.

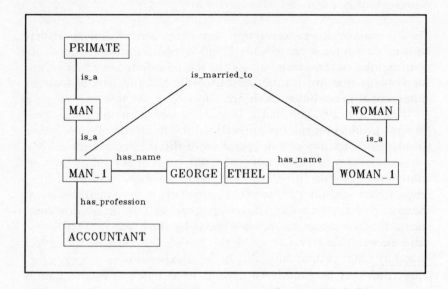

Figure 3.2 A semantic net.

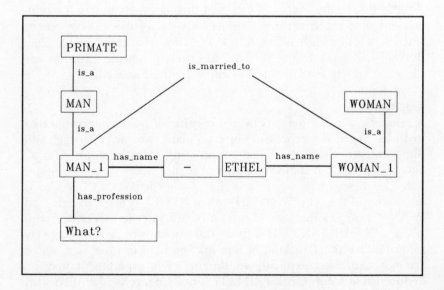

Figure 3.3 Reasoning in a semantic net.

The emulation of reasoning using semantic nets proceeds via a matching process. Thus, if one were to ask, 'What is the profession of the man that Ethel is married to?', then this query could be represented by Figure 3.3.

The 'what?' represents the identity of the object required. The '-' represents the identity of an object that is not currently known but which is not required. When this fragment is matched with the original network, the subject of the query (what?) becomes 'bound' (i.e. matched) to the value 'ACCOUNTANT' and the query is deemed to have been answered.

Object–Attribute–Value (OAV) triplets

In this method for representing knowledge, facts are associated with a triplet consisting of an object (e.g. car, bank loan), one of its attributes (e.g. colour, amount), and a value for that attribute (e.g. red, £1,000). An ensemble of OAV triplets may be considered as a specialised case of a semantic network in which there are just two kinds of relationship: has_a from object to attribute, and is_a from value to attribute.

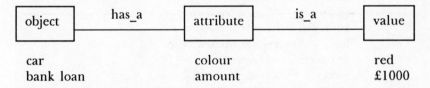

Sometimes production rules are couched in OAV terms. Here is an example from MYCIN (Shortliffe 1976)

> IF   the site of the culture is blood, and
> the morphology of the organism is rod, and
> the gram stain of the organism is gramneg, and
> the patient is a compromised host,
>
> THEN   there is suggestive evidence that the identity of the
> organism is Pseudomonas aeriginosa.

In this example the ordering is attribute–object–value (e.g. site-culture–blood).

Frames

A frame is a device for the identification of a concept in terms of its attributes and position in a class hierarchy. The attributes which are

also referred to as *slots* take on particular *values*. For example, a
specific computer audit question might be described by the following
structure:

> user specification question frame:

>> | area: | change_control |
>> |---|---|
>> | phase: | specification |
>> | context: | agent |
>> | text: | Do users participate throughout the amendment specification process? |
>> | answers: | Yes;No |
>> | risks: | none;specification error |

This is a specific instance of the generic computer audit question
frame which may be written as follows:

> generic computer audit question frame:

>> | area: | <area_value> |
>> |---|---|
>> | phase: | <phase_value> |
>> | context: | <context_value> |
>> | text: | <question_text> |
>> | answers: | <{answer_list}> |
>> | risks: | <{risk_list}> |

The 'slots' (area, phase, etc.) specified at the generic level are in-
herited by the instance at the next lowest level where they are given
the specific values which characterise the instance being considered.

3.2.2 The inference engine

The inference engine is, in principle, an application-independent
device which contains the procedures used for the manipulation of
the knowledge represented in the knowledge base. Assertions and the
relationships between them may be expressed in a variety of ways,
involving arithmetic, strictly boolean (or crisp) logic and several
styles of 'soft' reasoning, such as 'fuzzy' logic. The conclusions it
infers (from the knowledge structures and the user supplied answers)
are not necessarily certainties but can have a degree of probability
or likelihood associated with them.

Examples of the kinds of statement that an inference engine
can manipulate may be found in the following areas:

(i)   *Arithmetic*

      Net_pay = Gross_pay − Tax

Here Net_pay is computed using an arithmetic operation.

(ii)   *Crisp logic*

    IF   has_mortgage
    AND (mortgage_amount < 30000)
    THEN qualifies_for_full_mortgage_relief

In this example the assertions represented by:

    has_mortgage
    (mortgage_amount < 30000)
    qualifies_for_full_mortgage_relief

may take either the values TRUE or FALSE, and nothing in between.

(iii)   *Fuzzy logic*

    Tall people take long strides.

In this example the qualifiers 'tall' and 'long' are imprecise. A person may be tall to a greater or lesser degree. The truth of a person being tall is a continuous (as opposed to discrete) function of his/her height. Such an assertion is said to have a 'fuzzy value'.

    The order in which the assertions represented in the knowledge base are dealt with depends upon the *control strategy* used by the inference engine. Expert systems generally use either one or both of two control methods known as *backward chaining* and *forward chaining*.

    In *backward chaining* the truth of a goal (i.e. an assertion) is considered as dependent upon its component sub-goals, and so on until the lowest level 'goals' are but data asked of the user or read from a file. When operating under the backward chaining control strategy an expert system is therefore said to be 'goal driven'.

    Forward chaining is a control strategy in which an expert system is 'data driven', i.e. in which known facts or data are inspected, which then permit certain sub-goals to be satisfied which in turn permit the establishment of the truth of top level goals (i.e. conclusions).

The difference between the goal-driven and data-driven strategies may be illustrated by consideration of the following diagram (known as an 'inference net') which represents the logical connections between a variety of assertions.[1]

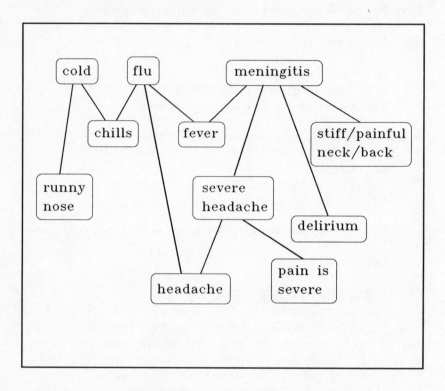

Figure 3.4 An inference net.

This diagram may be said to represent the following four rules:

Rule 1:   IF   the patient has a runny nose
            AND   the patient is suffering from chills
            THEN   a common cold is suspected

---

[1] The example is for illustrative purposes only and should not be taken as medically accurate.

Rule 2:   IF   the patient is suffering from chills
            AND   the patient has a headache
            AND   the patient has a fever
            THEN   flu is suspected

Rule 3:   IF   the patient has a fever
            AND   the patient has a severe headache
            AND   the patient has a stiff or painful neck or back
            AND   the patient is delirious
            THEN   meningitis is suspected

Rule 4:   IF   the patient has a headache
            AND   the pain is severe
            THEN   the patient has a severe headache

Two kinds of main enquiry may be put to an expert system containing this sample knowledge base:

(a) Does the patient have a particular condition?
(b) Given certain facts, what does the patient have?

These two kinds of enquiry are answered using backward and forward chaining, respectively.

To process the question 'does the patient have flu?' the inference engine first searches for the rule whose consequent is 'flu is suspected' since it is the establishment of the truth of this assertion that is the ultimate goal of the enquiry. Having found the rule in question (rule 2) the inference engine then takes each of the antecedents in turn and attempts to establish its truth. In the present case this would be done by asking the user of the system the questions: 'is the patient suffering from chills?', 'does the patient have a headache?', and 'does the patient have a fever?'. If all of these questions are answered in the affirmative then the truth of the assertion 'flu is suspected' will have been established. The reasoning here has been 'goal driven' or 'consequent driven' and has proceeded from the top level goals down to the level of the factual data, i.e. top-down.

An alternative way of using the knowledge base is to pose the question, 'Given that the patient has a runny nose, is suffering from chills, and has a headache, what could he be suffering from?'. In this case the expert system has been given a collection of raw data and is required to work up the inference net (bottom-up) from the data to the goals (data-driven or forward chaining).

The inference engine invokes (i.e. 'fires') each rule in turn and establishes the truth of those other assertions that it can. Thus, considering rule 1, since the assertions 'patient has a runny nose' and 'patient is suffering from chills' have both been established, it follows that the assertions 'a common cold is suspected' can be said to have been established. When considering rule 2, although the first two assertions of the production are established, the third ('the patient has a fever') is not, so the conclusion (i.e. goal) 'flu is suspected' must remain unestablished. Likewise, consideration of rules 3 and 4 does not lead to the establishment of any more conclusions.

3.2.3 The user interface

Expert systems are usually used in interactive mode and it is the user interface which is responsible for presenting the user with smooth, human-like responses. It is generally accepted that an expert system should be able to both explain why it is requesting particular (and perhaps costly) data and also justify how it has come to its conclusions.

The utility of an expert system is often seen in its ability to explain its reasoning, for without this the user would be forced into blind acceptance or rejection of its conclusions. In this context it is expected that the classes of explanation mentioned above will ultimately prove to be inadequate in the development of viable systems. The interfaces of extant systems generally suffer in the following ways:

- The structure of the generated dialogue is too rigid.
- The dialogue is always initiated by the system — i.e. a real change of initiative is not possible giving rise to a constrained dialogue which takes too long.
- The representation of the knowledge is highly coupled to the generated conversation.
- The explanations provided are generally only rule traces.

In real consultations, however (Kidd 1985):

- The consultant needs to be able to answer a range of question types, i.e.,
  (a) What constitutes a fault?
  (b) What constitutes the remedy?
  (c) Why did the fault occur?
  (d) Why did the remedy work?
  (e) Why didn't the remedy work?
  (f) Will another (specific) remedy work?

- The client is able to say what he is going to do, whereupon the consultant can respond with a critique of the client's intention,
- The consultant's explanations are fluent and are a function of the expert's view of the user.

The construction of the user interface is often reported as being the single most costly element in the development of an expert system.

3.2.4 Other architectures

Not all expert systems are of the consultative kind. They may operate in batch mode (e.g. DEC's XCON), or they may operate in real time (such as a process control system). In such cases it may not be possible to exercise a consultative function while the program is running.

A common architecture for real-time expert systems is the so-called 'blackboard' system which emulates a situation in which a group of experts stand around a blackboard (which represents a world view) and take turns to update what is written on it by virtue of the conclusions that they come to as a result of viewing the newly updated state of the blackboard. External sensor data are usually fed into the system (i.e. onto the blackboard) at some stage during an operative cycle. Such systems are commonly used for 'signal to symbol' processing, i.e. in the interpretation of digitised but real time data (Nii *et al.* 1982).

3.3 Classification

There have been several attempts at the classification of the different functions that expert systems have addressed. Any one chosen application is likely to contain elements of several categories no matter what classification scheme is chosen. A frequently quoted scheme is suggested by Stefik *et al.* (1982):

Interpretation The analysis of data to determine their meaning.
Example: The interpretation of geological data to aid mineral exploration.

Diagnosis The process of fault-finding in a system (or determination of a disease state in a living system) based on interpretation of potentially noisy data.

Example: The diagnosis of infectious diseases.

Monitoring   The continuous interpretation of signals including the
                setting-off of alarms when intervention is required.
Example: Real-time monitoring in a process control room to
                reduce cognitive overload on operators.

Prediction   Forecasting the course of the future from a model of
                the past and present.
Example: Predicting the effects of a change in economic policy.
                (Some planning programs have a predictive compo-
                nent.)

Planning   A plan is a programme of actions that can be carried
                out to achieve goals. Planning means to create plans.
Example: The planning of experiments in molecular genetics.

Design   Design is the making of specifications to create objects
                that satisfy particular requirements.
Example: Designing a digital circuit.

3.4   Examples

Some examples of expert systems are briefly described below to
indicate some of the areas in which they have been applied. The
systems discussed here were some of the first to be proven as technically, and in most cases, operationally and economically feasible.
Examples of expert systems that directly relate to accounting domains
may be found in Chapter 4.

DIPMETER ADVISOR is an expert system developed at
Schlumberger (Smith 1984) for the interpretation of oil-well logs
which are recordings made by specialised tools lowered into oil wells.
As the tool is raised it records various measurements associated with
its geological environment. For example, the dipmeter tool measures
the conductivity of the surrounding rock at regular intervals as it is
raised to the surface. From these measurements petroleum geologists
are able to make inferences about the structure of the geological
strata in the region of the bore hole. The DIPMETER ADVISOR
system is designed to reproduce the performance of a petroleum
geologist in the interpretation of these dipmeter oil-well logs.

MYCIN is a consultative expert system whose task is to determine the presence of an infection on the basis of clinical information about a patient. Its knowledge is represented in about 450 production rules and its control paradigm is backward chaining (i.e. it is a consequent driven production system). An example of one of the production rules used in MYCIN is reproduced below (Shortliffe 1976).

IF   the stain of the organism is gramneg
AND   the morphology of the organism is rod
AND   the patient is a compromised host
THEN there is suggestive evidence (0.6) that
         the identity of the organism is pseudomonas.

The '(0.6)' mentioned in the consequent is a certainty factor. An assertion which is associated with a certainty factor is interpreted as meaning 'certainly true' when the latter has a value of 1 and as 'certainly false' when it has a value of -1, intermediate values being interpreted according to their magnitude and sign. In this way MYCIN deals with missing or uncertain data through the propagation of certainty factors through its inference network.

XCON is an expert system that configures computer systems in the various ranges produced by DEC (McDermott 1982). The input to the system is a customer's order. XCON then checks the order for completeness and consistency and provides details about the modifications that have to be made to the order. The system then produces a number of diagrams showing how the various components on the order are to be connected and spatially associated. The task is characterised by a large set of constraints embodying a large amount of knowledge. Before the implementation of the system this task was performed by a human who would take about thirty minutes to complete it and be wrong about thirty per cent of the time. After the system had been developed and became used on a regular basis the same task would take about two minutes and errors would occur in only two per cent of the cases. The rules contained in XCON number about 10,000 and the knowledge base is maintained by a team of about ten full-time DEC employees. It is estimated that the system saves DEC in the region of $10 million per year.
Further examples of expert systems are presented in Chapter 4.

3.5   Utility

To a casual observer it may appear that expert systems are a recent
phenomenon. This is true in a purely commercial context, but research into expert systems has a thirty-year history. What appears
to have raised the commercial world's awareness with respect to this
aspect of artificial intelligence is a combination of two things. First,
the advent of ever-cheaper and faster computers has made feasible
the creation of programs which rely upon symbol manipulation for
their functioning — an impracticable possibility using previous genera-
tions of computer hardware. Second, the realisation that the successful
utilisation of software for the manipulation of knowledge is likely to
provide a competitive edge to those able to achieve it.

What are the principal advantages that the implementation
of expert systems confer over conventional systems, and to what
degree have these advantages been realised?

3.5.1   The promise

Distribution
The most immediate implication for a business that implements
expert systems is the ease with which otherwise scarce and costly
specialist knowledge may be distributed. Generally speaking, the
kinds of tasks that expert systems address themselves to are of the
routine variety, so that they are most applicable in situations which
require routine expert performance as opposed to creative expert
performance. It is therefore expected that copies of expert system
software would be useful at sites which would require access to the
kind of routine expertise described. In essence, this strategy would
enable generalists to inform themselves in a specialist area and avoid
bothering the expert with relatively 'silly' questions.

Availability
The knowledge that expert systems contain can be made accessible
at any time. This might have implications for expertise which might
be required at odd hours (for example, in the middle of the night
in a hospital) or in other time zones (for example, in a European
bank when the relevant expert might be sleeping somewhere in the
US).

Efficiency

So far we have considered the implications of the implementation of expert systems from the user's point of view, i.e. that they facilitate the spatial and temporal distribution of expertise. The expert himself, however, is also likely to benefit since the use of these systems, in making routine expertise more widely available, will have the effect of liberating him from spending time on relatively simple tasks. As a consequence the expert will have more time for the pursuit of the creative solutions required for those problems which demand more than just a routine approach.

Archiving

Human beings die or find other excuses for leaving and it is in the interests of a firm to find ways of retaining the rare expertise of its employees before they depart. Expert systems provide a way of doing this.

Standardisation

A problem that may concern a firm which employs a large number of semi-expert practitioners or consultants (for example, a law firm or an accounting office) is the lack of a common approach to consultancy. The use of expert systems may provide a means of aiding the standardisation of the professional services provided by the individuals in the firm.

Training

As well as being used in its standard 'expert assistant' function the knowledge base developed during the construction of an expert system may also be used to train novices in the domain of application. In principle, all that is required is to 'bolt on' the appropriate inference engine to the knowledge base depending on which function is required of the system. Given the distributable nature of expert system software the technology could form the basis of an inexpensive and efficient training approach.

Knowledge articulation

A largely unexpected bonus that is almost always experienced during the knowledge elicitation process is that as a result of his articulation of his expertise the expert becomes much more aware of his own knowledge, how it is structured and how he uses it. This generally has the effect of crystallising and formalising the expert's knowledge, so making it clear to him how he might become more effective in his task.

The training effect
Another unexpected (although unsurprising) effect of expert system implementation is that after a certain period of use, the user finds that he has become sufficiently familiar with the system's knowledge and no longer needs to use it. The user becomes trained in the domain of expertise even though this might not have been the original intention.

3.5.2 The reality

The starting point for the involvement of British industry in expert systems may be taken to be 1981 when the first expert system shell was marketed (SAGE by SPL International, now SD-Scicon). Since then the number of expert system software products appearing on the market has mushroomed but there still seems to be a dearth of reports about successful expert systems. What is happening? Let us consider some possibilities.

Businesses are loath to invest in such an unknown and therefore potentially high risk-area
This is almost certainly true of small businesses but the indications are that large amounts of money and other resources are being committed to research and development in this area by the very large industrial concerns. This would appear to be particularly true of the defence establishment.

Systems are being developed but their developers refuse to talk about them
In a recent report Alex d'Agapayeff (1984) strongly criticised industry for its secrecy about the developments which he discovered are taking place behind securely closed doors. The reason for this is the fear of losing a potential competitive edge through the publication of research results. The result is that the same wheels are continually being reinvented.

It is difficult to cost-justify an expert system development
There is a growing realisation that the development of a substantial expert system is very costly and that it is almost impossible to estimate the likely benefits. This means that even if management sanctions the appropriate commitment of resources and a system is built and is technically successful then it will still be some time before it is clear that the benefits of using the system will compensate its cost in a predictable time frame. Under these circumstances, it

would not be surprising if a company was reticent about advertising its involvement in expert system development.

Expert systems are much harder to build than was earlier thought
There is as yet no established methodology for the construction of expert systems, and the indications are that those elements which are recognised as likely to be part of any future established methodology are still largely research issues.

From those development experiences that have been published it is of interest to note the kinds of difficulty that expert system designers have come up against. A summary of some of these follows.

Unclear objectives
As implied above it is common for a company to expect a product when it should be asking for a research study. For development to be successful it has to be on the basis of a set of sound research findings. Academic institutions and software houses often seem equally naive, by accepting projects as development when they should be aware that the underlying research questions have not yet been explored.

Management and organisational problems
It seems to be the case, especially in the context of a commercial company, that an expert system project requires a champion to push it through. However, although this is a necessary condition it is not sufficient. What is also necessary is that the project is enthusiastically supported by higher management (for a detailed consideration of those factors influencing the likely success of such a project, see Chapter 6).

Knowledge acquisition problems
Feigenbaum *et al.* (1971) has described knowledge acquisition as the 'bottleneck' in the expert system design process. There is not yet an established methodology in this area and considering the delicate nature of the situation (a busy and possibly nervous and defensive expert being quizzed by a relatively inexperienced knowledge engineer generally ignorant in the area of expertise) the chances of a successful knowledge transfer are less than certain. Apart from the nature of the players themselves there may be organisational constraints on the degree to which the expert may cooperate, especially if the firm involved is nervous about exposing its knowledge.

The user interface
No matter how technically correct an expert system is, if it doesn't present a friendly face to its user it will gather dust in a corner of the office. It is consistently reported that the user interface is the single most costly and labour intensive aspect of expert system software production, typically accounting for 40 per cent of the effort. The art of the design of optimum user interfaces (together with what constitutes appropriate man–machine dialogue) is still in its infancy and it is to be expected that the general acceptance of knowledge-based systems will be predicated on the existence of user interfaces of very high quality.

Accountability
It is noteworthy that the most quoted expert system, MYCIN, which was designed for use in a hospital (it diagnoses for blood infections) is not used 'in anger'. The reasons for this are evidently that the medical personnel refuse to transfer responsibility to a computer program. However, MYCIN, is apparently extensively used as a training aid for novices. It may well be that training will be the major area of application in areas for which the responsibility for taking a decision is a particularly sensitive issue, as in medicine and law.

3.6   Tools for the Construction of Expert Systems

For a thorough account of this area the reader is advised to turn to one of many excellent existing texts such as Harmon and King (1985).

Expert systems are constructed generally through the use of one of three types of tool, namely AI *languages*, expert system *shells*, and knowledge engineering *tool-kits*.

By far the most common AI languages are LISP and PROLOG. LISP (from LISt Processing) has a particularly simple structure with only one data type – the list. Both programs and data are expressed as lists and this gives the language great flexibility. PROLOG (from PROgramming in LOGic) is a language based on the formal structure associated with so-called 'first-order predicate logic'. The inference process is driven by the laws of logic and proceeds via a method of matching symbols.

Using languages such as LISP and PROLOG, a system designer has a great deal of freedom in his choice of knowledge representation techniques and control strategies. However, use of these languages requires a high degree of expertise and skill.

In the first expert systems the inferential and domain specific parts of the program were mixed which made it quite difficult to change the system when some of the knowledge had to be updated or added to. As a result these systems were redesigned so that the inferential functions were separate from the knowledge functions. These two aspects of an expert system have come to be known respectively as the inference engine and the knowledge base. It became clear that an inference engine used with a knowledge base of one domain could equally well (so it was then thought) be used with a completely different knowledge base. Thus the idea of the *expert system shell* evolved — an inference engine with an empty knowledge base which must be supplied by the developer and written in a high-level language tailor made for the inference engine to operate on. The software also usually supports a user interface which provides such facilities as explanation, justification and traces, etc.

Generally speaking, shells are limiting unless the particular problem to be addressed fits very well. Shells tend to be 'solutions looking for problems' unless they are extremely flexible. But this is not to say that a shell may not be able to provide a cost-effective way of resolving problems requiring knowledge manipulation. Most shells support, to varying degrees, backward chaining, forward chaining, fuzzy logic, Bayesian updating, demons (actions which may be triggered at any time upon the satisfaction of a prespecified condition) and external file/system communications. However, most are not fast enough to operate in real-time and are therefore limited to producing the consultative type of expert system.

Tool-kits attempt to combine the flexibility of AI languages with the modularity of shells and provide more general development facilities than the latter. They are in general driven by high-resolution graphics user interfaces using windows, icons, mice, and pull-down menus (WIMPs). Because of their richness of functionality they tend to require a significant investment of time to learn before their full potential can be realised.

Chapter 4

Expert Systems Research and Development in Accounting

In this chapter we review the directions in which much of accounting-based expert systems research is taking and then provide a sampling of applications and developments in the accounting and finance fields.

4.1 Research

A limited amount of expert systems research is being performed in the UK by accounting practitioners or academics. Research in this area tends either to take place as part of the development process, and this only in the very large firms, or it is a sponsored academic activity, as indeed was the project that gave rise to this volume. The bulk of coherent accounting expert systems research is taking place in the United States and it is to this area that we now turn our attention.

Given the American reputation for generosity when funding research programmes it is to be expected that the US would be ahead of the UK in its accounting expert systems effort, and indeed this is the case. However, active though it is, this area also suffers a large number of constraints. US academic accounting departments seem to be inhibited because of the difficulty encountered by PhD students in gaining acceptance for expert systems research proposals as doctoral research topics. This seems to stem from the requirement of the established accounting academic community that doctoral research should be 'pure', together with the perception that expert systems research does not conform to this specification. The result is that students who would like to engage in expert systems research are often forced to submit proposals along more traditionally pure lines. This inhibiting mechanism seems to continue to have an effect until researchers have achieved tenured academic positions by which time they may indulge in whatever research they like during the limited time available after the execution of other professorial duties. This seems to lead to the result that expert systems research, as such, is, in the main, being performed only by people who have safely tenured positions, and then only on a part-time basis.

It should be emphasised that the above appears to be true of accounting departments, but not of management information departments, where the constraints are not so strict. Further, although the US research profile is not as high as expected, it is still a great deal more prominent than that in the UK, in terms of both the volume and the quality of the work being output.

Research into the construction of expert systems is a very recent addition to the activities of practitioners and academics alike. It is also an area that houses many sub-areas, each of which is worthy of investigation in its own right. It would be unusual for a single piece of research to address the whole spectrum of issues associated with expert systems development, and usually a researcher will concentrate on just one or two of the issues involved in a single paper. In what follows commentary on the phases of expert systems development has been derived from the sources available. The research headings covered are not exhaustive but represent only those interests of the researchers whose work is reviewed.

4.1.1 The accounting research context

Amer *et al.* (1986) classify computer and information systems literature into three categories:

(a) conceptual considerations in accounting/database systems design,
(b) electronic data processing (EDP) auditing techniques, and
(c) computer-based decision support systems.

They then divide EDP auditing techniques into manual and computer-based techniques and place the consideration of expert systems in the context of the latter. Amer's classification does not take non-auditing applications into consideration and this is a reflection of the extent to which expert systems accounting applications are currently limited to the auditing area.

4.1.2 Motivation

It is widely recognised that there are two approaches to AI research. The first is primarily concerned with the emulation of the cognitive processes of a human expert. The second is more concerned with the construction of high-performance problem solvers. Both of these approaches are reflected in the accounting literature.

Bailey *et al.* (1986) make a distinction between 'the application of AI technologies for product development purposes and for fundamental research'. He relates this dichotomy of motivation to its effect on the consequent research approaches: 'The primary focus of an expert systems research project is the creation of a theory of a single expert's decision making processes', whereas 'developmental activities are those whose aim is to use existing technologies to program a computer to find solutions to problems that no computer program has previously been able to effectively solve. The primary focus of developmental projects is not the creation of new knowledge, but the creation of efficient and effective problem solvers using extant knowledge.'

Hansen and Messier (1986) also recognise these two different, although not necessarily independent, reasons for constructing expert systems.

4.1.3 The nature of expertise

Central to the issue of building an expert system (especially if the cognitive emulation view is taken) is the nature of the thing that is being modelled, i.e. expert behaviour. This is generally referred to in a vague way in terms of the use of 'heuristics', 'rules-of-thumb', 'compiled experience', etc. Meservy *et al.* (1986) refer to a list of behaviours that characterise an expert. Thus, when given a task, an expert is likely to 'solve the problem, explain the result, learn, restructure knowledge, break rules, determine relevance, and degrade gracefully'. Johnson (1986) attempts to take a more formal view and distinguishes between the terms 'expertise' and 'expertness' and defines an 'expert' accordingly. Thus *'expertise* is a body of operative knowledge permitting the execution of a variety of tasks and often implying a "theory" for the action taken. When an individual's behaviour meets criteria of efficiency and proficiency in performing some tasks they display *expertness* in the performance of that task but not necessarily the *expertise* of those who designed to sequence of activities they have mastered. *Experts* are human beings who have *expertise* and display *expertness* in carrying out a task' (our emphasis). Johnson then goes on to discuss how expertise might be investigated.

4.1.4 Methodology

Johnson (1986) describes the investigation of expertise as progressing in three phases. In the first phase the 'operative knowledge which is necessary for the performance of a task' is identified, the result of which is 'a statement of the knowledge that must be computed if the task of interest is to be done at an expert level'. In the second phase, a 'process theory', which identifies the knowledge necessary for doing the task and describes the procedures for how this knowledge might accomplish it, is formulated and tested. In the third phase the process theory is exposed to a larger set of task examples as well as to additional tasks 'designed to test the generality of [the] knowledge introduced in the theory'.

Meservy *et al.* (1986) describe the methodology associated with the construction of his system (for the evaluation of internal controls) in two phases: discovery and verification. The discovery phase is subdivided into model development, and model implementation and tuning. In the context of a model for the evaluation of internal controls, model development comprised the elicitation of knowledge from experts consisting of the 'problem-solving steps and heuristics that represent auditor judgement in:

(a) identifying internal accounting control objectives,
(b) identifying controls and faults in the accounting system, and
(c) evaluating the system controls, weaknesses, and sufficiency of documentation'.

He then constructs preliminary representations of this expertise. Model implementation and tuning consisted of implementing the model in appropriate software and then running it through several standard case studies and checking its rules and lines of reasoning with an expert. During the verification phase the model was exposed more rigorously to a wider set of case studies and the results compared with the performances of other experts. The model's performance was examined for both the quality of its processes and also for the adequacy of its outcomes.

Bailey *et al.* (1986) discuss methodology in terms of what he calls the expert systems approach (ESA) to the investigation of human information processing. The ESA comprises four integrated stages:

knowledge acquisition, knowledge representation, computational modelling, and validation. Bailey accepts that 'experts can seldom accurately describe what they actually know and do in accomplishing their tasks' and therefore that '[t]his type of knowledge, which may include both heuristic knowledge and domain specific facts, is commonly referred to as tacit knowledge' and that therefore it 'must be elicited using indirect methods'. He discusses three kinds of indirect methods for knowledge acquisition:

(a) descriptive methods utilising interviews, lectures and written materials,
(b) observational methods which rely on process tracing techniques, e.g. protocol analysis, and
(c) intuitive methods in which 'the knowledge engineer becomes an expert and attempts to extract relevant problem-solving heuristics and domain facts from himself'.

Bailey then discusses knowledge representational issues and overviews the two main schemes being used in this area: production rules and frames. At the computational modelling stage the system designer must decide whether to use a programming language (e.g. LISP, PROLOG), an expert system shell (e.g. EMYCIN, GALEN), or a representation language (e.g. OPS5, ROSIE) to implement the model. Each of these choices has disadvantages. Using a programming language entails starting from scratch; using a shell commits the design to a particular framework; and using a representation language involves mounting a significant learning curve. Finally, the model must undergo validation (see section 4.1.6 below).

Hansen and Messier (1986) discuss the development of their system EDP-XPERT as having progressed in two phases, as follows:

Phase One
1.1 Reviewed research literature
1.2 Consulted EDP audit manuals
1.3 Interviewed experts (computer audit specialists) from firms
1.4 Established an appropriate AI structure for the representation of the experts' knowledge

Phase Two
2.1 Performed knowledge acquisition with the experts
2.2 Identified a software package appropriate for problem domain
2.3 Developed an initial prototype system.

There then follows an extensive evaluation exercise which should really be considered as the third phase of development.

In describing the construction of the system AUDITPLANNER Steinbart (1987) distinguishes three steps: (1) the choice of a particular software tool, (2) the selection of a subject, and (3) the development and refinement of the knowledge base.

Steinbart reports that EMYCIN was chosen as a tool but does not actually say why he thought this choice to be most appropriate for his application. During the second step eleven major accounting firms were screened and a single subject was chosen on the basis of whether they regularly made and quantified planning-stage materiality judgements (the chosen application area), and whether those judgements were made on the basis of an expert individual's professional judgement rather than from the application of a general algorithm.

The development of the system's knowledge base proceeded in three steps: first, the construction of an initial working prototype using the firm's audit manuals; second, the use of interactive sessions with the expert using the prototype with real case studies in order to modify and tune the knowledge base; and third, the formal evaluation of the model using six other auditors and thirteen other case studies.

Shpilberg's case study (Shpilberg and Graham 1986) is of special interest because it describes the construction of an expert system in a commercial environment. Shpilberg organises the process as follows:

Phase 1: Knowledge engineering: Designing the product's environment
1.1   Understanding the expert system's tasks
1.2   Exploring product delivery environments
1.3   Identifying the experts
1.4   Defining the structure of the knowledge base
1.5   Distilling technical requirements
1.6   Selecting software and hardware

Phase 2: Knowledge acquisition: Building the knowledge base
2.1   Selecting the experts
2.2   Interactive knowledge acquisition
2.3   Enhancing the system shell
2.4   Knowledge base validation

The spirit behind this approach resembles that associated with conventional commercial software development practices. The first phase constitutes a very thorough investigation into the proposed environment of the system and is conducted before any of the system construction activities are begun.

4.1.5 Knowledge acquisition

Probably the most difficult aspect of expert systems development is the process of gaining access to the knowledge which is to be encapsulated into the system, known as knowledge acquisition or knowledge elicitation. A number of approaches or techniques may be used as aids to knowledge acquisition and they may or may not involve interaction with domain experts. These include the gleaning of information from textbooks and manuals as well as the use of structured interviews, repertory grid analysis, teach-back techniques or protocol analysis with the cooperation of experts. In the US a great deal of knowledge acquisition research centres around protocol analysis. The seminal texts for this approach are Newell and Simon (1972) and Ericsson and Simon (1984). Generally speaking, this approach requires that the expert 'think aloud' while performing an expert task. The knowledge engineer conducting the knowledge acquisition interrupts as little as possible during the process and the near monologue is tape-recorded and transcribed. The resulting protocols are then analysed, the details of the analytical techniques used being determined by the specific objectives of the researcher. This approach is tedious and extremely labour-intensive.

Bailey et al. (1986), Klersey and Mock (1986), and Meservy et al. (1986) all discuss or use protocol analysis as a research method. Bailey discusses protocol analysis in the general context of process-tracing methods and concludes that in spite of criticism against it, there is as yet nothing better. Klersey and Mock (1986) address the problems involved in attempting to arrive at a set of common codes for protocols for use in process tracing research. The idea here is to provide a common basis upon which different research studies may be cross-validated. Meservy et al. (1986) use protocol analysis extensively in the construction of a computational model for internal control evaluation. Their detailed study describes how the protocols of both experts and the computational model are coded and analysed for cross-comparison during the evaluation phase of model development.

Other authors (Grudnitski 1986, Hansen and Messier 1986, Steinbart 1986) have used published documentation, either alone or as adjuncts to a later interview technique for knowledge acquisition. Hansen and Messier (1986) report that an initial protocol analysis exercise failed to produce production rules for the system's knowledge base and that they were subsequently obliged to revert to searching available hardcopy for the system's prototype knowledge base.

A novel approach is presented by Shpilberg *et al.* (1986), in which the *modus operandi* of the envisaged expert system is simulated by arranging for an individual representing a typical user to be seated at the same table as but separated by a curtain from two experts with whom he may communicate only verbally. The individual is provided with a case study for analysis together with all appropriate documentation and with licence to consult the experts across the table. The ensuing dialogue is taken as a model for a typical expert system consultation and an appropriate knowledge base is then derived by close analysis of the generated transcript.

4.1.6 Validation

The task of testing expert systems software (assuming that some computational model has been implemented) contains an extra dimension compared to the comparable task in the conventional software world. All of those aspects of software testing/validation that are relevant to conventional systems are also relevant to expert systems, but with expert systems there is an additional concern with the 'performance' or the 'behaviour' of the system when compared with that of a human. Conventional computer programs transform data in a highly predictable and tightly specified fashion. What is unusual about knowledge-based software is that the space of resultant data configurations is very large and, as yet, there are no known methods available for exhaustive testing. This is not surprising since one of the driving forces behind the development of AI techniques was the development of automated heuristic methods designed to effectively constrain very large solution spaces.

The literature being reviewed considers two approaches to the validation of expert systems corresponding to the principal motivations for their construction. If the cognitive emulation attitude was adopted then the emphasis for validation would be on the comparison of the process traces generated by the system with those of a human expert. If, on the other hand, the motivation for the creation of the system was the construction of a high-performance problem-solver then the emphasis during the validation stage would be on the quality of the outcomes.

Bailey *et al.* (1986) distinguish three stages of validation:

(a) comparison of the model's outcomes with those of the original expert,
(b) comparison of the model's outcomes with those of several experts, and
(c) the introduction of normative model elements to enhance the model's efficiency.

In this study Bailey *et al.* emphasise the expert system as problem solver.

Hansen and Messier (1986) take a similar approach but refine the problem-solver validation task by defining two approaches for achieving this: (1) reproducing the 'correct' answer, or (2) reproducing what a human expert states is the correct answer. They then accept that the first of these is not generally available and so settle for the second.

Johnson's (1986) approach to validation was to distribute testing procedures between the second and third phases of his research methodology. The second phase was divided into discovery and verification stages. During the verification stage the proposed model was tested and evaluated by presenting it and a set of human experts with a series of new test cases. The solutions thus generated were then presented (blind) to a panel of different experts. The model's performance could then be calibrated against the performances of the human experts.

In Johnson's third phase of research, case study data sets were systematically and artificially perturbated and fed to both the model and to human experts and subsequent behaviours were compared. When he did this Johnson found that the model and the humans made the same mistakes.

In Meservy *et al.* (1986) detailed study the verification phase consisted of evaluating his computational model from both the point of view of the quality of model processes and from that of the sufficiency or adequacy of model outcomes.

Shpilberg *et al.* (1986) validated their system by presenting it to a group of practice partners and managers in different offices and asking them to test the system for a representative set of their clients.

4.1.7   Applications

Five application areas are represented in the research being reviewed:

(a)   Internal controls evaluation (Bailey *et al.* 1986, Grudnitsky 1986, Johnson 1986b, Meservy *et al.* 1986)
(b)   EDP controls evaluation (Hansen and Messier 1986)
(c)   Going concern judgement (Biggs and Selfridge 1986, Dillard and Mutchler 1986)
(d)   Tax accrual and planning (Shpilberg and Graham 1986)
(e)   Materiality judgement (Steinbart 1987)

Messier and Hansen (1986) also mention applications for (1) assessing the adequacy of a client's allowance for bad debts, and (2) assisting auditors in assessing bank loan loss reserves.

4.1.8   Application assessment

A critical preliminary issue that must be addressed before building an expert system is whether or not the proposed application domain is suitable. Not much comment was discovered regarding this during the current review. The single exception was provided by Messier and Hansen (1986) who quoted Duda and Gaschnig (1981) in stating the conditions necessary for the successful development of an expert system. This issue is sufficiently important for these conditions to be restated here:

(a)   There must be one human expert acknowledged to perform the task well.
(b)   The primary source of the expert's exceptional performance must be special knowledge, judgement and/or experience.
(c)   The expert must be able to explain the special knowledge and experience and the methods used to apply them to particular problems.
(d)   The task must have a well-bounded domain of application.

Messier and Hansen add a further six conditions to these four:

(e)   The completed system should be expected to provide a significant benefit to the organisation.
(f)   If the problem primarily involves numerical computation, other methods may be more effective.

(g)   The potential users of the system should be enthusiastic about the product.
(h)   There must be an appropriate measure for assessing the quality of the expert system's judgements.
(i)   The skills required by the task should be teachable to novices.
(j)   The need for the expert system should be expected to continue for several years.

The reader is recommended to Prerau (1985) for a comprehensive treatment of how to assess a proposed application for the suitability of development into an expert system.

4.1.9   Cost

Another important aspect of expert system construction that was generally not addressed in the papers reviewed was the cost of producing such a system. The only authors who mention the issue, even in an indirect way, are Shpilberg and Graham (1986). They state that for the development of ExperTAP, 1000 hours of expert time were required. No mention is made of the knowledge engineering personnel commitment necessary for the transformation of this expensive expert time into a viable product.

4.1.10   Summary

A situation in which commercial interests are pressing expert systems developers to come up with usable and profitable products has given rise to a vibrant and creative tension between the practising and academic communities. One expects development whereas the other prefers a more cautious research approach. The result can be exciting as well as confusing. Nevertheless there is concern, especially in the United States, about the status of expert systems development work as research. Bailey *et al.* (1986) has however gone a long way towards explaining how the development of such systems may be considered as an integral and important aspect of a pure research approach.

The principal research interests current in the US academic accounting community include a preoccupation with such issues as the nature of expertise, the effectiveness of protocol analysis as a process-tracing technique, the cognitive behavioural characteristics of the accountant (the auditor in particular), and the problem of designing appropriate metrics for the evaluation and verification of the cognitive models that are created.

All of these areas of interest impinge directly on the central practical issue of how to build an expert system and are therefore as vital to practitioners as they are interesting to academics.

4.2 Development

This section reviews accounting-oriented expert systems developments. The reader will notice that not all the systems quoted are operational but represent a spectrum from 'research' through 'under development' and 'prototype' to 'working'. The range of systems presented here provides the reader with a good idea of the general state of accounting-related expert systems at the time of writing the book, although it should be noted that this aspect of the study may date fairly quickly.

4.2.1 Criteria for inclusion of a system within this review

Adopting a functional approach requires a definition of the boundaries of the accountancy function. Expert systems that tackle the traditional accounting tasks such as auditing and tax advice clearly need to be included. The audit function is likely to become an important area of exploitation for expert systems; to date the literature shows seven systems having been built in this area. Each deals with only a limited subset of the audit function and is in no sense an 'automated auditor'.

Taxation systems also seem likely to be popular. Many firms spend a high proportion of their time dealing with the interpretation of tax rules as they apply to a particular client's circumstances. Clarke and Cooper (1985) reported in their survey that

> any simplification of the tax system would reduce the
> amount of work [available]. For one practice, written and
> telephone communication with the Inland Revenue repre-
> sented 60% of all their external communication.

An activity that is lucrative and labour-intensive, as well as apparently rule-based, seems an ideal candidate for an expert system. A number of systems have been developed, each in a limited tax domain.

The provision of what might be described as 'financial services' also merit inclusion. Although the boundaries here are less distinct between accountants, banks, and others, activities such as investment advice and corporate financial planning are undoubtedly an integral part of present-day accountancy. Such plans may relate to a specific project, such as a new product or service, or they may embrace a wider horizon, such as a redirection in business emphasis, perhaps in terms of an acquisition or merger. Three financial planning systems are included in this review.

4.2.2   Details of accountancy-oriented expert systems

Expert systems reported in the literature may be categorised under four functional headings:

(a) audit and internal control systems,
(b) taxation systems,
(c) financial planning,
(d) interpretation of (non-tax) regulations,

Table 4.1 gives examples of systems currently developed in each functional area, showing each system's sub-domain. An indication is given of how the system was or is being constructed and its present state of development at the time of writing. The systems are ordered chronologically within sub-domain group.

In the following sections, each system is described, giving the following information where possible:

• a short functional description of the system,
• its operational environment,
• the anticipated user,
• an indication of how the system was or is being constructed,
• its current state of development.

4.3   Auditing Systems

EDP-EXPERT

The domain
An audit requires an assessment of the way in which a client uses and maintains computing equipment. As computing equipment has fallen in price, its use has proliferated. The rigid control exercised over earlier (often centralised) computer systems is no longer as

straightforward to maintain over decentralised or distributed systems. The task of auditing control procedures for such systems is usually performed by computer audit specialists. It is this expertise which EDP-EXPERT seeks to model.

Table 4.1 Expert systems in accountancy

Sub-domain	System name	Current status	Tools used	Reference
Auditing	EDP-EXPERT	prototype	AL/X	Messier and Hansen (1984)
	TICOM	working	PASCAL	Bailey *et al.* (1984)
	AUDITOR	working	AL/X	Dungan (1985)
	AUDITPLANNER	research	EMYCIN	Steinbart (1986)
	CFILE	prototype	NEXPERT	Willingham *et al.* (1986)
	CheckGaap	working	C	Pattenden (1986)
	ICES	prototype	EMYCIN	Grudnitski (1986)
Taxation	TAXMAN	prototype	LISP	McCarty (1977)
	CORPTAX	prototype	BASIC	Hellawell (1980)
	ACCI	working	ADVISER	Roycroft and Loucopoulos (1984)
	TAXADVISOR	working	EMYCIN	Michaelsen (1984)
	TA	working	PROLOG	Schlobohm (1985)
	DIRECTORS-TRANSACTIONS	prototype	CRYSTAL	Evens (1986)
	EXPATAX	U/Dev	APES	Cunningnham (1986)
	ExperTAX	working	LISP	Shpilberg and Graham (1986)
	PAYE	prototype	PROLOG	Torsun (1986)
	VATIA	working	C	Susskind and Tindall (1988)
Financial planning	CASHVALUE	product	BASIC	Ash (1985)
	FINANCIAL ADVISOR	product	LISP	Bernstein (1985)
	PLANPOWER	product	LISP	Apex (1986)
Government grants	GRENSIDESE	prototype	SHELLS	Gambling (1984)
	GGA	prototype	TESS	Evens (1986)
Risk management	ALFEX	U/Dev	PROLOG	ALVEY Reps (1986)
	CIRAX	prototype	CRYSTAL	Edwards (1986)

The system
Three senior computer audit specialists provided the expertise, supplemented by knowledge from other sources such as text books and audit manuals. In its initial form the system had about sixty rules and a single overall goal — the reliability of the control system. After testing the system was then restructured to include four separate goals — the reliability of supervisory, input, processing and output controls. These modifications have increased the size of the knowledge held to 133 rules. In use, the system poses questions relevant to a particular goal selected by the user, who responds using a numerical value to represent strength of certainty. The system uses these responses to advise on the adequacy of client controls, using a method similar to that mentioned in AUDITOR above.

The user
The intended user of the system is the senior computer audit specialists. The system is seen as 'a problem solver not an expert emulator' (Hansen and Messier 1985).

Development tools
The system was built using AL/X.

Current state of development
The system is beyond its initial stage of development. However the developers see a need to widen their validation procedures using a greater number of (costly) computer audit specialists. An expansion of the knowledge base to include on-line and database systems is also envisaged.

TICOM

The domain
Review of internal control procedures is a familiar audit task, typically carried out by interview and observation and recorded using traditional flowcharting techniques and reports.

The system
TICOM, developed by Bailey *et al.* (1985) at the University of Minnesota, is a computer-based system which imposes upon the review process a predefined structure allowing a model of the internal control procedures to be built. This structuring helps in the evaluation of completeness and consistency in the control procedures, and

allows the auditor to interrogate the system about aspects of internal control.

The system operates in two phases. The first phase requires the user to enter details of the internal control procedures using an internal control description language. The second phase allows the user to interrogate the system using a query-processing language.

It could be argued that TICOM is not an expert system. It contains no general domain knowledge such as that which an expert might possess. Its knowledge is specific to each single application. However, it can be seen as an important precursor of auditing expert systems.

The user
The system is seen as an aid for practising auditors.

Development tools
The system has been built in Pascal using a CDC Cyber 720 computer.

Current state of development
TICOM was seen as a possible first step towards an auditing expert system. The control system would be modelled using TICOM and the controls could then be evaluated using the expert system. The system had reached version 3 by April 1985.

AUDITOR

The domain
AUDITOR is an expert system which provides assistance in the auditing task relating to the assessment of allowance for bad debts (ABD). Such allowances are calculated initially by clients and it is the task of the auditor to make a judgement upon the reasonableness of the ABD, in the light of data about the debtors, the age of the debt, etc.

The system
AUDITOR was developed by Dungan and Chandler (1983). Eight expert auditors assisted in the compilation of twenty-five rules, each of which contributed to the goal: determining whether or not the outstanding amount should be reserved for in the ABD. These rules are represented as an inference network, with links within the network represented by user-defined weights. The system poses questions

and the user responds, expressing the strength of certainty numerically.

For example, a question such as, 'how certain are you that recent collections towards the delinquent portions of this account are proceeding satisfactorily?' might be answered by entering '5' (certain or absolutely true) or '−5' (very uncertain or absolutely false). These weights or certainty values (CVs) act upon the single overall goal of the system, the validity of the ABD, affecting the 'degree of belief' (DB) in the goal. The higher the DB of the overall goal, the stronger is the suggestion that the debt should be allowed. The system also enjoys the facility of allowing the user to volunteer information at any time rather than merely to reactive passively to the system's promptings, thus avoiding the need to answer questions which, for a particular audit, are perhaps less significant or irrelevant.

The user
The system is designed for use by auditors in the field. This is reflected in the nature of the dialogue and the apparent terseness of query facilities. Some technical expertise in navigating one's way around the system is also desirable. The authors admit, for instance, that 'to volunteer information one must know the internal name of the associated rule', not the sort of knowledge a casual user might retain.

Development tools
AUDITOR was built using AL/X, from Intelligent Terminals Ltd of Oxford.

Current state of development
The system, originally developed on a Cyber mainframe, has been adapted for operation on an IBM PC or compatible. The authors have tested the system with live data, and are currently addressing the problem of a 'non-polarised' treatment of ABD: situations where the delinquent amount is partially allowed for, rather than being either allowed or disallowed.

AUDITPLANNER

The domain
There are no hard and fast rules regarding the roles of materiality judgements in the audit process. It is very much a matter of judgement based upon experience and an appreciation of the circumstances

of the case in question. Materiality can influence the planning of an audit and the evaluation of audit evidence. It is the planning judgement that AUDITPLANNER seeks to model. It is therefore concerned with ensuring that the evidence collected during the audit will be timely, relevant and sufficient.

The system
The system was built using textbook knowledge, which was then modified during interactive sessions with an audit partner who had a wide variety of experience in making planning-stage materiality judgements. The current knowledge base has about 100 rules. The system chooses a materiality base guided by inferences it makes about the interests of financial statement users. The system uses certainty factors to qualify its conclusions. Percentage rates for calculating materiality are suggested and if circumstances exist such that the system perceives there to be an increased business risk, the system modifies percentage rates accordingly.

The user
The system is seen as a piece of research to gain insight into materiality judgements, and therefore the user is seen as another auditor whose views might differ from those embodied within AUDITPLANNER. In use, the system may show why there is a lack of consensus among auditors in this area.

Development tools
The expert system shell EMYCIN (Van Melle 1979) was used.

Current state of development
The project is seen as a stage in the development of a taxonomy of materiality judgement models. There is a need therefore to develop other models based on the views of other individual auditors.

CFILE

The domain
CFILE is concerned with bank audits. In the USA a variety of banks perform in specialised areas. Specialist expertise about the audit of such banks is not always available. A particular problem for the auditor is loan loss evaluation; estimating the amount of reserve required to cover the bank's current loans.

The system
The user is asked details about the size of loan, security held and period of loan. Depending on the answers to these questions the system goes on to ask further questions until it has sufficient data to make a judgement on the amount of reserve necessary. Questions may be asked in an abbreviated form to suit experienced users. It is also possible to carry out sensitivity analysis to assess how the response to a particular question might influence the reserve conclusion.

The user
Possible users may be seniors with limited bank audit experience.

Development tools
A micro-based commercially available shell was used. It is hoped to transfer the system to a new shell NEXPERT shortly.

Current state of development
Results so far obtained indicate that the model performs well on straightforward cases but that as the complexity increases (that is, user judgement becomes more important) so the model's performance dips. Work is continuing to deepen the knowledge base and to incorporate weighting factors based upon the source and recency of data.

CheckGaap

The domain
Once an audit report has been prepared, it requires careful checking to ensure it complies with the UK Companies Act. To assist in this procedure, auditors at Deloitte, Haskin and Sell compiled an eighty-page checklist, but found that its length meant it was seldom used. CheckGaap is an automated version of this checklist.

The system
The user is guided through a tree structure enabling an inspection of only those aspects of the legislation relevant to the audit report in question.

The user
The user is the auditor-in-charge at the client's premises, typically a second- or third-year student.

Development tools
Deloitte's team built their own shell, Browse, using C and Assembler. The system runs on an IBM PC.

Current state of development
The system is operational.

ICES

The domain
ICES is an internal control expert system that focuses on sales/accounts receivable transactions. The system is designed to give assistance during the preliminary evaluation phase, during which the audit team typically assesses the likely adequacy of existing controls to determine the extent and need for substantive testing.

The system
The system evaluates a hierarchy of objectives relating to internal controls. The user is asked to supply information about the existence of controls relating to sub-objectives, the fulfilment of which contributes to an overall objective of adequacy of controls. The system then makes recommendations concerning the effectiveness of controls.

The user
The system will provide support for members of audit teams who lack experience in making internal control judgements.

Development tools
The expert system shell EMYCIN (Van Melle 1979) was used.

Current state of development
The system is still in the prototype stage. It is hoped that its construction will facilitate the process of knowledge elicitation in the internal control environment.

4.4   Taxation Systems

TAXMAN

The domain
Tax rules govern liability to tax of gains resulting from corporate reorganisation. 'Despite the apparent precision of these rules, the courts have intervened repeatedly throughout the history of the [IR] code to deny a claimed re-organisation status to transactions which have seemed inconsistent with their underlying purposes or assumptions' (McCarty 1977, p. 846). TAXMAN was developed to perform 'rudimentary legal reasoning' (McCarty 1977, p.838). In this respect it is a model of the law, rather than an individual's expertise.

The system
TAXMAN allows the relevant facts in a particular case to be represented as a semantic network. A match is then sought between these facts and the circumstances associated with one of the six types of corporate reorganisation (types A to F) allowable under section 368 of the US Internal Revenue code. More than one match can exist; the reorganisation could qualify for exemption on a number of grounds.

The user
In view of its pioneering nature, and its emphasis on legal reasoning rather than expert advice , it is hard to judge TAXMAN fairly on its use in its reported form. McCarty, however, was quick to recognise that TAXMAN, or an extension of it, could perhaps be used to plan an organisation's strategy with regard to possible future taxation liability — much more an 'accountancy' than 'legal' function: 'the user could describe an initial situation and a desired end result and then generate a number of possible transaction patterns with the desired tax consequences' (McCarty 1977, p. 888). It could be argued that this is more a modelling process than advising. It could also be argued that it is *expertise* that is being modelled. A key question is whether such a system behaves functionally as an expert.

Development tools
The system was developed between 1971 and 1973 by McCarty at Stanford, mainly using micro-PLANNER (Sussman *et al.* 1970), although some parts were written directly in LISP, giving a total of about 650 lines of code. The system ran on a PDP-10, typically

taking less than thirty seconds to produce a result (McCarty 1977, note 90, p. 876).

Current state of development
TAXMAN was built more than ten years ago. McCarty's work continues in this area.

CORPTAX

The domain
Like TAXMAN, CORPTAX models the law rather than the expertise of particular individual(s). Its domain is Section 302(b) of the IR code, which is concerned with whether a stock redemption qualifies for favourable tax treatment.

The system
The system performs four functions.

(a) It acts as a checklist, ensuring the user seeks all the relevant information from the client.
(b) It performs any calculations necessary to reach a judgement.
(c) Where the law is clear, it acts as a repository of the law in this area.
(d) Where the law is unclear, it can cite and refer to precedents and give an opinion on whether the redemption qualifies for favourable treatment.

The user
The system is designed for use by lawyers although one can envisage its use by other classes of tax planner.

Development tools
The system was written in BASIC PLUS to run on a DEC System 20 minicomputer.

Current state of development
Although the system is completed, Hellawell (1980) suggests a number of directions (in terms of other statutes) that lend themselves to similar analysis.

ACCI

The domain
The Finance Act 1972, Schedule 16, empowers the Inland Revenue
to apportion the income of certain companies, called close companies,
amongst their shareholders, thereby ensuring that certain wealthier
shareholders do not avoid payment of tax on dividends. This piece
of legislation is invoked rarely and is complex. ACCI (apportionment
of close companies income) is a system to assist tax inspectors with
this legislation.

The system
Knowledge was acquired using Inland Revenue training notes, statutes, the tax inspector's field manual, and by interviewing an expert.
A conceptual model was constructed, from which the knowledge base
was built. The knowledge is held as rules.

The user
The system was designed for tax inspectors who do not specialise in
apportionment.

Development tools
The system was built using the shell ADVISER running on an ICL
2900 series computer.

Current state of development
The system deals with those cases which in the inspector's view merit
closer examination. A large number of cases are filtered prior to this
stage and a possible extension of the system might model this filtra-
tion process.

TAXADVISOR

The domain
TAXADVISOR operates in the domain of financial planning for an
individual and his or her family, sometimes referred to as estate
planning. It is designed for individual rather than corporate clients.
Michaelsen (1984) sees a logical approach an expert might adopt to
provide assistance in this domain as:

(a) initial screening, to assess if the client's circumstances warrant an
    expert's help;

(b) gathering information on which to base recommendations;
(c) reconciling the client's wishes and circumstances, thereby determining a set of actions, eliminating those which appear in the
light of heuristics to be economically unsound;
(d) subject the set of actions to economic analysis, producing a final
set of recommendations.

Michaelsen concludes that an expert system in this domain ought to
concentrate on steps (a) to (c). The system ought to 'maximise the
wealth that an individual transfers at death', which in practical terms
he sees as 'recommendations that are regarded as an acceptable
exercise of expert judgement as evaluated by a majority of experts'
(Michaelsen 1984, p. 152).

The system
The system is designed to guide the user through its knowledge,
which is held in the form of 275 production rules, acquiring data to
fill gaps in its knowledge as the session develops. Certainty factors
indicate strength of belief in a response: where a positive or negative
response needs to be moderated, the user can enter a value between
1 and 9 to indicate this.
    The system first seeks to eliminate unsuitable clients, by
enquiring into their circumstances. If the client's suitability is confirmed, the system assesses the client's circumstances based upon six
consultation sub-domains: estate insulation, premature death, retirement, lifetime planning, gifts, transfers at death. The system ensures
that the client enjoys protection against unexpected catastrophes
before attempting to formulate longer term plans. Finally, when each
of the six sub-domains has been considered, the system gives a list
of recommendations. The system was validated by external tax experts
using double-blind procedures.

The user
The system is designed for users with some knowledge of the domain,
perhaps a 'general practitioner' in the taxation field. It is not designed for client use, nor to be useful for every client.

Development tools
TAXADVISOR was built using EMYCIN (Van Melle 1979). The
system runs on a DEC 10. A full consultation typically takes thirty
minutes.

Current state of development
The system was built in 1982.

TA

The domain
TA (Tax Advisor) advises in the domain of actual or constructive ownership of stock, as regulated by Section 318(a) of the United States IR Code. Constructive ownership may be interpreted as, for example, where a child's or grandchild's stock is considered for tax purposes to be 'owned' by the parent or grandparent. Although Section 318(a) gives rise to little if any uncertainty, its unravelling is often tedious.

The system
TA assesses constructive and actual ownership of shares by interrogating the user about his family, business partners and their shareholdings. The system offers explanation facilities although often these simply refer back to Section 318(a).

The user
Considerable effort was made by Schlobohm to 'permit a user who is not a computer expert to use the program . . . more effort has gone into devising a suitable user interface than into the more complex issues of representing the rules and knowledge required to implement the Section 318(a) programs'.

Development tools
TA was written in PROLOG-86 to run on a Compupro micro.

Current state of development
The system was written in response to an AI programming competition for a practical application on a microcomputer. Shortcomings in the 'Help' facilities, due partly to hardware constraints, are acknowledged by its author.

DIRECTORS-TRANSACTIONS

The domain
Like TAXMAN and CORPTAX, this system is concerned with company law, in this case those sections of the 1985 Companies Act

relating to the legality of loans to directors. This domain was chosen for its conciseness.

The system

The system interrogates the user on the nature of the loan, determining which sections of the legislation apply. The session is menu-driven and makes good use of windowing. Explanation and query facilities are easy to use, and it is possible to navigate through the knowledge. There are thirty-five rules of the 'IF–THEN' variety.

The user

The system was developed by Arthur Young as an exercise in assessing whether a domain expert might build his or her own system, although in view of the straightforward nature of the system, a specialist from a different sub-domain would find it easy to use. Like TAXADVISOR, it could be used as a filter, prior to directing a client to the appropriate domain expert.

Development tools

The system was initially built using Xi (Expertech 1985), but was later transferred to Crystal (Intelligent Environments 1986). Both shells run on the IBM PC. The system took the domain expert approximately eight days to build.

Current state of development

The system was developed as an experiment. At present there are no plans to develop it further.

EXPATAX

The domain

The system holds knowledge on statutory law, Inland Revenue statements of practice and other public domain material on a narrow but complex area of UK taxation.

The system

The system has approximately 400 rules. The user is presented with a series of menus which that guide him through the knowledge. The system questions the user, also by means of menus, to satisfy goals. The user is able to query the system about its conclusions or line of questioning.

The user
The system is seen as having both tutorial and advisory functions.

Development tools
The system was built using the shell APES, taking about six man-months to reach its current state.

Current state of development
The system is still under development.

ExperTAX

The domain
Tax accrual and tax planning are two separate but related aspects of the audit (the ExperTAX system could equally well have been included in the Audit systems section). The tax data collected during the audit forms the basis of both accrual and planning functions, although audit staff assigned to the data collection may not realise the tax planning implications of some of the data, resulting in relevant data not being collected.

The system
ExperTAX guides the auditor through the information gathering process ensuring that relevant data is sought. The system analyses the results highlighting those which need to be brought to the attention of audit and tax managers. The system was constructed using over twenty experts, each providing different expertise such as knowledge of what questions should be asked, how they should be asked, how the answers should be interpreted, and what strategies arise from the interpretation. This led to a knowledge base of over 1000 frames. Frames in ExperTAX are of two types. A question frame gives details of a question, its antecedents, a list of possible answers and explanatory text which is displayed upon request. An issue frame has associated with it a rule and a display. When the rule is true, the text is displayed. During consultation the user enters the required information by responding to menus. Questions may be skipped for later completion and the user has a facility for entering notes at any time. At the end of the consultation the system produces accrual and planning reports, together with a list of all questions, responses and notes made during the session.

The user
Field use by the audit senior.

Development tools
In view of its intended use, the system was designed to run on an IBM PC or compatible. A purpose-built shell was used, QShell, as it was felt that existing shells were too inflexible and too slow.

Current state of development
The system appears to be in an operational state.

PAYE

The domain
Taxation of employees income is most often carried out by using the pay as you earn (PAYE) system, which is regulated by government tax legislation. This legislation changes frequently, and the large body of formal rules needs to be augmented in practice by knowledge of the effects of time and events together with case histories.

The system
The system can give advice either in a general tax advisory capacity or relating to the tax problems of specific situations or individuals. The system models the PAYE tax rules, together with legislation regarding National Insurance contributions and statutory sick pay. The knowledge was created using tax documentation, with recourse to Inland Revenue experts where necessary. The system interfaces with other employee databases during consultation. The user is then presented with a set of conclusions upon which to act.

The user
The system was designed to assist or replace a PAYE expert within an organisation.

Development tools
The system was built using PROLOG and will interface with INGRES relational database and COBOL database files.

Current state of development
The system is still under development.

VATIA

The domain
Value-added tax (VAT) is a UK tax on the supply of goods and services, making it applicable to almost all business operations within the UK. Although there is no statutory requirement on the auditor to ensure that a client's business complies with current VAT regulations, many general auditors will undertake a review as part of the annual audit.

The system
The objective of the system is to assist the general auditor in assessing the adequacy of clients' compliance systems and procedures. The system is divided into seven modules each representing an aspect of VAT. The modules include registration with HM Customs and Excise (who administer the tax in the UK), completion of returns, input and output tax, and the keeping of records. The system is largely menu-driven, with an average consultation taking between one and two hours. The consultation is terminated by the production of a report summarising key areas of concern identified during the consultation.

The user
The system was designed for use by the general auditor, with the summary report being reviewed by a senior member of the audit team. A 'help' system is available and it is envisaged that the system will serve a valuable training role in addition to its operational audit use.

Development tools
A prototype was developed using a standard shell. The operational system is based upon an amended version of the shell, programmed in C. It was a system requirement that the operational version run on IBM PC or compatible.

Current state of development
The system went into operational use for its developers, Ernst and Whinney, in May 1988.

4.5   Financial Planning Systems

CASHVALUE

The domain
CashValue's domain is capital project appraisal, which embraces cash flow, project valuation, and risk evaluation.

The system
The user provides information on the type of project and its location, together with other general information about how the project will be structured. The system prompts the user for forecast figures that can be entered in nominal (i.e. today's value) or real (i.e. inflation-indexed) terms. The system produces cashflow summaries for the project based upon the user's input. These summaries may take the form of post-tax net cash flows, allowance schedules, tax calculations, working capital adjustments, final year wind-up effects, etc. The system also uses discounted cash flow techniques to calculate economic statistics such as net present value, as well as performing the various sensitivity analyses familiar to financial spreadsheet users.

The system uses a knowledge of the rules of capital budgeting, together with various financial planning heuristics. Advice is given in the form of a consultancy report in plain language identifying possible discrepancies between the project and the system's knowledge of real world applications.

The user
CashValue is designed for financial managers, drawing upon the user's knowledge of finance rather than computing.

Development tools
The system was developed by Heuros Ltd, and runs on an IBM PC. It is written in BASIC and took eighteen months to develop.

Current state of development
CashValue is a 'product' costing around £700.

FINANCIAL ADVISOR

The domain
The system offers advice in the broad area of capital allocation and budgeting, contributing to the analysis of mergers, acquisitions and other business opportunities.

The system
Details of the system are not available. It will probably gather its data from diverse sources such as external databases, requiring proportionately far fewer inputs from the user than other systems reviewed above. The output of the system will probably be a high-level management report.

The user
Users are expected to be chief accountants or financial directors of major companies.

Development tools
The system requires a LISP workstation in addition to links to other mainframes.

Current state of development
The system is available from Palladian Software Inc. at a cost of $95,000. Its current users are operating as test sites.

PLANPOWER

The domain
PLANPOWER contains knowledge covering some of the areas considered in earlier sections of this report, for example taxation advice, including investment and estate management, as well as retirement planning. In addition, risk management and cash and credit management can be analysed.

The system
The system incorporates a database and a spreadsheet facility as well as the conventional inference engine and knowledge base. It contains 'the equivalent of 6000 rules and detailed knowledge of more than 125 types of financial products' (Expert Systems 1985). The system takes a client through each of the six sub-domains mentioned above, making recommendations about each. The system also includes

actuarial tables and demographic data. The system is menu-driven, with the spreadsheet facility allowing a degree of 'what-if' modelling. Among its novel features is the facility to produce the system's findings and recommendations in the form of English text, with word-processing capabilities should amendment be necessary.

The user
PLANPOWER is designed for institutional users such as banks or accountancy firms, who will use the system to produce a comprehensive financial plan for individual or corporate clients.

Development tools
The system was written in LISP by APEX Inc., who used a panel of domain experts over a period of three years. The software runs on a Xerox 1186, which is an integral part of the system.

Current state of development
PLANPOWER is a 'product' currently available at a cost of about $50,000, including the hardware.

4.6 Interpretation of (Non-Tax) Regulations

GRENSIDESE

The domain
The system holds knowledge on 'profit for non-competitive government contracts', and is concerned with the proper apportionment of overheads and expenses for costing such contracts. The rules for what is or is not acceptable have been laid down by the review board for government contracts, after the chairman of which the system is named.

The system
Pilot systems have been built using a variety of shells and environments. Menus are used, with users able to moderate their strength of certainty in the answers.

The user
The Ministry of Defence (MOD) is the main contractual partner on the government side. Envisaged users are those who deal with the MOD, particularly small contractors who have insufficient resources

to employ accounting staff, or 'first-time' contractors who do not know the ropes.

Development tools
The developers experimented with a number of environments.

Current state of development
The system is at the outline design stage. Knowledge about the *interpretation* of the regulations, rather than the regulations themselves, are a possible future enhancement.

GGA (Government Grants Adviser)

The domain
Grants are available for certain types of business activity. GGA attempted to assess whether such grants were applicable.

The system
The objective of the system was partly experimental, to develop a better understanding of the knowledge acquisition and representation processes (see also DIRECTORS-TRANSACTIONS above, which had similar objectives). The user is guided through the system, with use made of menus and windows.

The user
The users were expected to be accountants.

Development tools
The system was built using a shell, TESS, running on an IBM PC.

Current state of development
The work was carried out for the Alvey Directorate as a joint project, with Arthur Young providing the domain expert and Helix Expert systems the knowledge engineer. The project has now ended.

Chapter 5

Future Developments in Expert Systems for the Accounting Profession

5.1 Introduction

In this chapter the future of accounting expert systems is explored. Such explorations are always dangerous; the literature is littered with examples of crystal-ball gazing in which the kindest thing one can say about the predictions is that they are best forgotten. As Nils Bohr ruefully observed, 'It's difficult to predict, especially the future' (Feigenbaum and McCorduck 1983). Like all wise speculators, we will try to hedge our bets, by looking at the events of the recent past in the hope that they may inform us of the near future. Of the more distant future, we will offer no possible scenarios, only likely directions for both research and development.

To achieve this objective, this chapter is structured as follows. First, the responses of our survey sample are summarised, and compared with the predictions of other authors who have assessed the potential impact of changes in IT on the accounting profession.

Second, we consider some of the ways in which expert systems may affect firms which decide to implement them, using as a framework for this investigation a rationale which might be offered by a sceptic for *not* introducing expert systems. We offer some reasons for the prevalence of this rationale, if not a justification.

Finally, we take an optimistic view of the ways in which firms might proceed with the introduction of expert systems into their organisation based on the bold, but perhaps not unwarranted, assumption that expert systems *will* find an important niche in the profession. We examine some of the effects of their implementation on the relationship of firms with their competitors, their clients, and on their own internal structure.

5.2   The Profession's View of the Future of Expert Systems

The detailed questionnaire (see Appendix C) sought the views of those who were already committed to the development of expert systems. In parts 4 and 5 of the questionnaire, respondents were asked to rank likely future developments and to gauge the magnitude of their impact on the profession in the immediate and longer term. Details may be found in the appendices, but the small sample size should make the reader cautious about extrapolating too enthusiastically. In summary, however, it can be said that audit is the area of most likely immediate application, followed by taxation, yet the impact of these applications is most likely to be in the latter rather than the former. The greatest impact, it was felt, would be in increasing the efficiency of existing tasks rather than easing the introduction of new tasks, although overcoming existing skill shortages was seen as having a significant impact.

Clarke and Cooper (1985), in identifying the likely future impact of IT systems in general (rather than expert systems in particular) on the accounting profession, suggest four types of change that would affect the profession:

• changes to the nature of the work carried out by accountants, such as the IT demands of clients would become increasingly sophisticated, requiring a level of IT knowledge beyond that possessed by most firms, possibly encouraging them into joint or cooperative agreements with software houses;
• changes to, or additional, external services, such as IT consultancy and training;
• changes to, or additional, internal systems, such as project planning and management software, more sophisticated billing and personnel systems, and electronic mail systems;
• changes to organisational (i.e. staff) structure; for example, the shortage of staff with IT skills may limit growth, lead to greater specialisation, a reduction in the grades below partner, and possibly an increase in homeworking (although elsewhere in their study this is qualified as being unlikely to become common before 1995).

Clarke and Cooper make little mention of expert systems, although it is one of four areas singled out by their respondents as being thought of as likely to be commonplace by 1995. It could be argued that the three years since their survey represents a significant passage of time in IT terms, and one might have expected to begin to see increased evidence of such systems in use. Our surveys indicated an increased awareness rather than an increased use. The responses seemed to sum up the profession's attitude to the future of expert systems as 'interested, but not yet convinced'. In the next section we try to establish whether the profession is dragging its heels, or being wisely cautious.

5.3 How Will the Future Use of Expert Systems Change the Firm that Uses Them?

The motivation for using expert systems is fundamentally a business one. What will expert systems offer that no other technology can give? To remind ourselves of some of the benefits we mentioned earlier, what they have to offer is:

* the promise of a new technology that can store and distribute knowledge and offer advice based upon such knowledge,
* a means of archiving skills that are rarely used, or in danger of disappearing from the organisation,
* an interactive training medium of possible use to junior members of staff, particularly in the acquisition of technical skills,
* an 'on the job' assistant for junior members of staff, particularly in the context of skills beyond their accustomed day-to-day use,
* provision of guidance through rule-based situations such as applicability of legislation, allowances, etc.

The problem with all of the above is that they are relatively untried and untested, certainly within an accounting context. It is not clear that these benefits are actually achievable, or whether they will be outweighed by their costs. For many of the early success stories in other domains, the cost of research and development was not always laid alongside the benefit arising from the system's use, for the reasons suggested in Chapter 3. Amongst other things, neither the cost nor the benefits may be easy to measure. The following section examines in more detail some of the objections which might be raised to the implementation of expert systems.

5.4   The Sceptic's Questions

Any new development represents an investment that will consequently be denied to an alternative, competing project. The decision to make such an investment was clearly one which the majority of our survey respondents did not believe the benefits merited. In considering the likely future of expert system development, we need to speculate upon the scepticism of most of the profession. In the eyes of the sceptic, the development of full-scale expert systems may be clouded by a number of objections, which can be summarised under the following headings:

(a)   Why bother?
(b)   Why not wait?
(c)   What application areas are most appropriate?
(d)   How much will it all cost?
(e)   How will the system be built?
(f)   What will be the effects of implementing such systems?

Although the last of these issues is the primary concern of this chapter, the first five contribute to Chapter 6. Let us briefly state a case under each heading.

(a) *Why bother?*
This position questions the underlying relevance of expert systems to business, at least in the non-technical areas in which much of an accountant's work lies. The objections generally posed are:

- Expert systems are merely a flash in the pan. They have no real future other than in very specific and limited applications and it is questionable whether their merit warrants the investment of resources.
- Expert systems are nothing new (so why all the fuss?). They are merely a different sort of decision support system (some of the literature we mention in Chapter 2 certainly supports this view) and as such represent a branch of a technology which we already have well under control.
- Expert systems cannot contribute anything valuable to the business, as there appears to be little financial benefit to be derived from their use. Once again, the literature could be used to support this argument, at least for accounting applications.

(b) *Why not wait?*

An accusation often levelled at the accounting profession is that it is conservative, reacting to change rather than precipitating it. However, the profession's attitude towards computing does not entirely support this view. Historically, the accounting department was the nursery of computing for most large organisations and although this function may now have been devolved to a data processing (DP) manager, the use of DP systems for the accounting function is still deep-seated, resulting in a willingness to adopt technological changes at least as fast, and perhaps a good deal faster, than many other professions. The growth in the use of microcomputers and associated software, particularly spreadsheets, would seem to bear this out. However, it is generally agreed that there is some financial advantage in not being an early leader in the field of any new technological development. The market place may not be ready for the product, and therefore it is generally considered that there is a greater risk in developing what may turn out to be unprofitable or unattractive offerings. Here we need to distinguish between systems built for use by the profession (internal systems) and those that might be built by the profession for their clients. The rationale for the former will be to provide a competitive edge, for the latter to keep abreast of clients or to demonstrate a position at the leading edge of IT development.

(c) *What application areas are most appropriate?*

Assuming entry into the field is thought to be desirable, the choice of application area can be critical. The literature on domain selection is not totally in tune with what appears to be happening in the profession. In most of the applications we have examined in Chapter 4, more weight seems to have been given to rules of thumb such as readily accessible expertise, the existence of an addressable 'problem', and the importance of organisational commitment. However, a wrong choice of application can be disastrous; the authors are aware of at least one example (not in accountancy) where an inappropriate choice significantly set back an organisation's overall expert systems development.

(d) *How much will it all cost?*

As with any innovative venture, it is difficult to estimate costs which may be weighed against benefits. Comparisons with traditional DP systems, whilst they may be a useful starting point, may not provide a very accurate guide. There is a shortage of first hand experience, particularly within the profession. Most successful systems have been in the technical and scientific areas (Buchanan 1986) making cross-domain comparisons dangerous. Published reports may have a tendency to exaggerate benefits, for a variety of reasons.

(e) *How will the system be built?*
There are three components to this complication: (e.1) software —
what software will be used? (e.2) hardware — what computing facilities
will be required? and (e.3) volksware — who will build it?

(e.1) *Software*. Most organisations have, for their larger systems at
least, a considerable investment in the traditional DP languages. As
was demonstrated in Chapter 3, procedural languages suffer some
drawbacks as tools for expert system development. Fundamentally
different programming concepts are associated with non-procedural
AI languages (for example predicate calculus with PROLOG, list
processing with LISP). There are problems associated with the familiarity of staff with these concepts, and the difficulty of integrating
programs written in these languages with other more traditional
software, e.g. COBOL, spreadsheet packages, etc.

The need for dedicated machines (for example, reduced
instruction set (RISC) architectures) to support these languages is
diminishing in significance, partly due to the reduction in cost of
such machines, and partly due to the growing availability of alternative compilers, particularly for microcomputers (Turbo-PROLOG has
become one of the fastest selling microcomputer software packages,
at a cost of £70 (Source: *Practical Computing*, November 1986)).

However, the more expensive expert system environments
provided by products such as KEE, ART, and ESE may require
dedicated hardware, but may be necessary if a firm is intending to
produce larger systems. Such a level of expenditure is difficult to
justify in an exploratory situation and is usually prohibitive for
run-time versions. This introduces the additional problem of porting
to a more economical delivery machine.

The choice of an expert system shell, which might prove a
cheaper alternative, is complicated by the growing number of shells,
their alternative inferencing mechanisms and their limited track
records. Many are easy to use, but like all software packages they
suffer from varying degrees of inflexibility, and are often limited by
their ability to adequately represent knowledge and by their usability
within a particular application. Some permit a degree of integration
with other software, allowing data to be transferred between the shell
and other packages such as Wordstar, Lotus 1-2-3, dBase III, etc.

One way of bypassing the problem of choosing a shell is to
build your own domain-specific shell. This is the course of action

adopted by Coopers & Lybrand (QShell), Deloitte's (Browse), and others.

All operational computer systems require documentation to facilitate their update and amendment. Expert systems are no exception, irrespective of what software is chosen for the system. Most accounting expert systems described in the literature are prototypes, often built by small, stable development teams for whom documentation may be a low priority. This situation will change with the development of full-scale systems, and so far only limited progress has been made towards the adoption of appropriate documentation systems which will need to be developed and maintained.

(e.2) *Hardware*. The hardware problems associated with expert systems relate to speed, cost, compatibility and graphics capabilities. If expert systems are to make a significant impact, each will need to be addressed.

Expert systems of any significant size, say more than 200 rules, soon become constrained in their use by the *speed* of machine response. An operator in the field would perhaps be looking for an acceptability level of about 5–10 seconds, which may be difficult to achieve even with enhanced-memory IBM PCs. The development of RISC architectures, or the advent of new machines to fill the gap between micro- and minicomputers, such as the Compaq, may only serve to complicate matters initially. So called 'dedicated' AI machines and Symbolics, Apollo and Sun workstations are already favoured by some organisations for their fast processing ability. More traditional computer manufacturers such as DEC and IBM are offering mini- and mainframe computers supporting AI languages and environments (e.g. OPS5, LISP and PROLOG, as well as environments mentioned above) which will operate at a tolerable speed.

Problems of *compatibility* relate not only to systems internal to a firm but also to client organisations' systems. Although software is available to provide a bridging facility between most manufacturers' hardware, future expectations might include integrated expert systems which, for instance, retrieve and inspect data from clients' own files.

The *cost* of hardware only becomes a significant problem if the development software chosen cannot be adequately supported on existing hardware. Thus for the development of small expert systems, typically PC based, hardware cost is not significant. Machines capable of supporting the environments and larger shells mentioned above range in price from £10,000 to £50,000+. As with software, the benefits of such systems need to be very clear before such a level of expenditure is contemplated.

Most commercial expert systems developed to date make little or no use of *graphics*, possibly leading to the conclusion that text-based systems are sufficient for business use. This view is supported by our survey responses, which suggest that there is little or no demand for enhanced graphical capabilities, nor for non-keyboard input media such as mouse or touch-screen. However, as the technical problems of knowledge elicitation, representation and inferencing are gradually overcome or by-passed, the need for alternative input and output methods may become more apparent, particularly in non-numerical environments.

(e.3) *Volksware.* The availability of appropriately trained staff presents a number of short-term problems for any organisation about to construct full-scale expert systems. The shortages are of knowledge engineers (broadly equivalent to systems analysts) and system builders (broadly equivalent to programmers). Although it is possible to train in-house to meet these shortages, it is arguable whether there is any substitute for first-hand experience when it comes to knowledge engineering, and there is also a general feeling that non-procedural programming languages are more difficult to acquire if the trainee has already acquired a knowledge of procedural languages (whose techniques need to be 'unlearned'). There is no empirical evidence for this view, however. In addition, the suppliers of some of the more sophisticated software tools (e.g. KEE, ART) insist that they should only be used by trained staff.

The use of external consultants to bypass skills shortages suffers some disadvantages. As well as the obvious expense, the track record of firms is often vested, in view of the infancy of the technology, in very few members of the firm, many of whom are becoming increasingly attractive to 'head-hunting' competitors. Even with reputable consultants, the clients must expect to be funding, directly or indirectly, a certain amount of research for which they might receive little or no benefit.

There are also manpower constraints with regard to the use of experts' time. Even assuming experts are available, their involvement in the project may represent a significant opportunity cost for the system's developer. The experiences of Coopers & Lybrand in building ExperTax, involving over 1,000 hours of experts' time, seem to reflect those of other system builders and may even be conservative if one considers the greater emphasis that might be placed upon user involvement in system development.

Finally, maintenance costs must be considered. DEC employ ten people full-time to maintain XCON (Sell 1986). These ongoing costs will eventually greatly outweigh development costs, if they have not done so already. The distinction between the two might become blurred as the very nature of expert systems makes the definition of the point marking the end of the development and the beginning of maintenance difficult to determine, but this does not diminish the importance of maintenance costs.

Table 5.1 Possible effects of expert system implementation and their relationship to strategic changes.

	Internal effects	Effects on competitors	Effects on clients
Changes in internal strategy (e.g. internal efficiency changes?)	Increased efficiency? Change in attitude by key staff? Reorganisation leading to reduction in autonomy?	Little or no effect? Increased perception of threat?	Focal point for expert system development
Changes in competitive strategy (e.g. moves within the profession?)	New business practices (e.g. audit?)	Maintain 'high-tech' reputation among competitors? Increase pressure on competitors? Emergence of new rivals?	Reduction/change in fees? 'Tie' clients to a firm by increasing switching costs Effects on internal auditors? 'High-tech' reputation?
Changes in portfolio strategy (e.g. changes in business)	Functional reorganisation? Recruitment policies? Staff training?	New competitors? Change in relationships with existing business partners?	New clients? New business with existing clients?

(f) *What will be the effects of implementing such systems?*

Perhaps the single most problematic issue when considering whether
or not to develop expert systems is the effect wrought by their implementation. This effect is likely to impinge upon three sets of
relationships: internal relationships, the relationship with clients, and
the relationship with competitors. Each of these relationships needs
to be reflected in the chosen corporate strategy. With regard to the
application of any new technology, Bakos and Treacy (1986) suggest
that this strategy is a combination of three complementary strategic
views:

- Internal strategy, which is concerned with how the organisation
  structures itself to best achieve its objectives in the light of technological changes.
- Competitive strategy, which focuses upon the inter-relationship
  between the organisation and existing or potential competitors.
- Portfolio strategy, which is concerned with appraisal and possible
  repositioning of an organisation's current business activities.

It is possible to try to assess some plausible outcomes of changes resulting from these three strategies by mapping them onto the
respective internal, competitive and client relationships to form the
matrix shown in Table 5.1. Each cell in the matrix indicates the
likely effect on competitors, clients or the firm itself from adopting
different emphases of change in corporate strategy. The following
section comments upon each element of the matrix in turn.

5.5   Possible Effects of Expert System Implementation and their Relationship to Strategic Changes

5.5.1   Internal effects of expert system implementation

Internal strategic changes may lead to internal reorganisations. Many
of the larger firms are already divided into a number of functional
areas such as audit, taxation, small business, management consultancy, each with some degree of autonomy, although there is movement
of staff between functions. The expertise resident in expert systems
may be scattered throughout the organisation, and this may not be
strategically appropriate or optimally effective. The level of internal
awareness, at all levels of the organisation may not best be served by

a fragmented approach, particularly when serious expert system applications are considered.

Competitive strategies may dictate a change in the way that traditional tasks are performed. Changes in audit practice, for example, are already being brought about by increased use of fileinterrogation software. Changes in fee structure, both internal and external, may be necessary. The organisational lack of expertise in expert systems might necessitate changes in recruitment or training policies. Particularly, staff may find a heightened need for computer literacy. Firms may find that, once the appetite of staff has been whetted for micro-based job aids, demand for them will increase.

Strategic changes in the portfolio of business activities may lend weight to the need for functional reorganisation, at least as far as the need for a multi-disciplinary yet focused approach to expert systems. As with competitive strategies, this may have implications for recruitment and training of staff. If, for example, a movement towards the provision of turnkey expert systems is envisaged, some expertise in the construction, development, testing and possibly maintenance of such systems will need to be offered to clients.

5.5.2 Competitive effects of expert system implementation

Changes in internal strategy are unlikely to affect the relationship with competitors, other than the extent to which increased efficiency may result in more competitive quotations for some aspects of the business. Any internal reorganisation may also signal to competitors an organisation's intentions within the market place, leading to an increased perception of threat.

Effects on competitors will be most apparent from the implementation of a competitive strategy. A division between the 'haves' and the 'have-nots' of expert systems expertise is more likely to be important for clients than competitors, although the possibility of staff movement between the big firms may become more apparent as shortages of special skills are perceived. Whether this movement is significant will depend upon the volume and value of business available and the number of competitors wishing to share in it. There is also the need for a firm to maintain its professional standing in the eyes of its peers, particularly in segments of the market where it is perceived to be at or near the forefront. A firm with a 'high-tech' profile may wish to continue to be seen as a technological innovator.

The prevalence of expertise in limited but specific domains may also have an effect on the competitive threat of some smaller accountancy firms. Although such firms may not previously have been considered serious competitors to the larger firms, expert systems will provide the ability to purchase a cheap and accessible desk top 'expert', where previously they might have needed to either refer the work on, buy in human expertise, or devote so much time as to make the service prohibitively expensive.

The competitive effects of changes in portfolio strategy may bring firms using expert systems into competition with new business rivals. This may have a more profound effect on the client–firm relationship, which will be dealt with in the following section. However, there is the possibility that institutions such as banks, with whom accounting firms often have reciprocal business arrangements (at least informally) may become competitors when armed with appropriate expert systems, although domains will probably be very limited, perhaps restricted to areas such as personal taxation or advice on legislation regarding small businesses.

5.5.3   Effects of expert system implementation on client relationships

Internal strategies will only affect clients to the extent that the increased efficiency they promote will be passed on to clients in terms of reduced fees or enhanced level of service. The centralisation of expert system expertise may represent a useful focal point for clients, particularly for new business or general enquiries. This may be equally valuable for in-house enquiries, although perhaps less necessary.

The extent to which client relationships will be strengthened by expert systems will depend largely on the success or otherwise of their implementation. It will be important to ensure that success is measurable and clearly understood by the client. The experiences and contribution of the consultancy side of some of the larger accounting firms ought to prove valuable in such a scenario. Competitive edge may be gained in the following ways:

(a) By introducing existing clients to expert systems, providing that the introduction proves satisfactory. This has the advantages of reinforcing existing goodwill, as well as demonstrating a 'high-tech' profile which may provide useful spin-off in other business activities, for example audit or management consultancy.
(b) By supporting clients in developing their systems, which might give some scope for influencing clients to build or implement systems in a manner that may prove beneficial to the firm as well as the client. This strategy may even extend as far as 'tying'

clients to a particular philosophy or product that might make switching to an alternative auditor or consultant prohibitively expensive.

The implications of the above for portfolio strategy may mean that expert system expertise may lead to a more involved relationship with some existing clients. If systems are developed for use by internal auditors, for example, then existing relationships may need to be reviewed. If a firm decides to produce an expert system 'product' it will need to train clients in its use. Alternatively, the training function may be much less specific, concentrating for instance on the more general 'management awareness' issues in expert systems.

The relationship between the firm offering such services and the new expert system software houses will also need to be established. Are they to be viewed as competitors, collaborators, or even as potential new clients?

5.6 Some Optimisic Pointers for the Future

In the following section, each of the objections raised by the sceptical questioner is addressed, and in each case an optimistic view of the likely impact of expert systems is proposed.

5.6.1 Why bother?

Successful applications in other domains have demonstrated that expert systems can contribute significant savings but only if appropriately used. Generally speaking, this means addressing a current business problem that is proving intractable to solution by conventional means. For business applications, the most useful attribute of expert systems is their ability to assist in the interpretation of complex rule based relationships and it is important that applications are chosen which best exploit this facility. An alternative strategy, that of applying expert systems to create opportunities rather than resolve problems, has generally received a less favourable reception by experts in the field. In any event, the consultancy role adopted by most accounting practioners (irrespective of the firm's size) makes the acquisition of expert systems expertise an important priority if only because expert systems represent another weapon to be added to the armoury with which to attack business problems. On these grounds alone it may be unwise to have a knowledge that is only superficial. The best way to acquire deeper knowledge may be to experience it at first hand, and to be seen by clients to have done so.

5.6.2   Why not wait?

A loss of initiative in expert system development may not be important in terms of the expert system market, but may be very important in reducing a firm's profile. To be considered amongst the leaders in the field can be important for the larger practices in maintaining a desirable public image for other aspects of the IT business, particularly consultancy.

It may be argued that a good reason for delay is the current relatively crude state of development tools. It is an inevitable feature of the high-technology marketplace that there is always something better 'just around the corner'. Any expertise acquired in constructing expert systems would not be wasted, whatever tools were being used. Even negative experiences could be usefully passed on to clients. A reasonable strategy for many firms might therefore be to proceed as soon as possible with a number of small, well defined projects, if only as a valuable learning experience.

5.6.3   Which application?

In light of the criteria offered for the assessment of a proposed expert system development (see Chapter 6), a firm needs to decide if the priority is to develop and use systems in-house, develop systems for clients, or to offer consultancy services only.

In-house applications that conform to these criteria should be capable of development to a usable state quickly, must be seen to be useful, and their use must be encouraged to ensure the pay-back benefit that the application of the criteria will have highlighted. Because quick development is important, such systems would almost certainly need to be shell-based.

For clients' systems, even the more experienced system builders may need to stress the exploratory nature that is likely to be the hallmark of larger systems, which even 'experienced' expert systems houses have found very demanding (the Alvey projects, for example).

As with any computerised information system, benefits will need to be carefully predetermined and capable of measurememnt, to minimise ambiguity over the success or otherwise of the application. However, there ought to be a preparedness to accept that some of the benefits may accrue from a detailed analysis of the expertise rather than from the output of the system.

The third option, that of offering only consultancy advice in this area, must surely be of limited appeal to most firms. There is no doubt that some income may be earned from sifting potential applications and recommending shells. However, some first-hand experience in the development and use of such systems might reasonably be expected by clients.

5.6.4   How much will it cost?

For immediate applications, costs can be minimised by using relatively cheap expert system shells such as those discussed in Part Two, which run on existing hardware. Development costs for in house projects could possibly be set against future consultancy fee income from selling-on the expertise gained. Full-scale projects could be developed either on a collaborative basis with a single industrial or commercial partner, or ideally on a fee-earning basis.

Costs involved in the setting up and marketing of a centralised expert system facility must also be considered, as must the possible need to recruit staff with appropriate skills or to train them. This will be less problematic for in-house systems, but may become acute for external systems, particularly large-scale or 'flagship' systems.

5.6.5   How will the system be built?

(a) *Software*. The expert system surveys (Appendices B and C) demonstrated that shells offer a cost-effective solution to the problem of building useful systems quickly. In Part Two of this book a shell-based approach to constructing a complex system is considered in detail. One of the limitations of shells until recently has been their inability to integrate comprehensively with other software. This limitation need not be inhibiting for the development of a firm's early exploration into expert systems.

(b) *Hardware* is unlikely to be considered in isolation from software. Most shells have a version capable of running on a PC/AT, and such hardware is often the delivery standard for firms, particularly if the system is to be used in the field. Shells are also available for mainframe development. For most firms, dedicated hardware is neither necessary nor desirable. As a firm evolves a more strategic view of the implementation of ESs, particularly the development of integrated systems, more consideration will need to be given to hardware compatability.

(c) *Volksware*. Attracting staff with appropriate experience in system development will be no less of a problem for expert systems than for traditional systems. *The Price Waterhouse IT Review* (Grindley 1988) regularly highlights the difficulties of staff recruitment and retention in its annual assessment of problem areas in IT. Many firms will encourage the growth of in-house expertise, possibly by following the example of some of the developers of ESs identified in Table 4.1.

5.6.6   What will be the effects of implementing such systems?

(a) *Internal changes*. The reorganisation of expert systems development into a centralised activity has already been mentioned. Such reorganisation is likely to have three effects. First, it will signal an organisational commitment to expert systems which clients may find reassuring, and may therefore prove to have some consultancy value. Second, it will provide a focal point for expert system enquiries and so enable a closer monitoring of the potential expert system marketplace. Third, it will act as a breeding ground for expert systems expertise within the firm.

If a decision is made to provide a full expert system service (perhaps even the provision of turnkey systems), rather than purely consultancy, then the organisational implications of such a strategy may need to be accommodated within a centralised framework.

(b) *Competitive changes*. The experience of building a large or successful system can result in a firm getting a good deal of valuable publicity as well as the actual knowledge gained from building large expert systems. Although many of the early accounting systems were experimental and non-competitive, there is more recent evidence to suggest that at least two or three systems in the US are at a level of development which makes them much more of a competitive threat. Systems such as PLANPOWER in the area of personal financial services, FINANCIAL ADVISOR for corporate financial services, and ExperTax for tax planning during audit, are beginning to be used competitively. PLANPOWER boasts 100 users, and Coopers & Lybrand are distributing ExperTax to 96 offices in the US. If the construction of a substantial system proves successful, then such success can be used as a foundation upon which customer confidence can be built. Going into collaboration with an industrial or commercial partner, possibly an existing client who is interested or has a problem, may further strengthen a firm's competitive position, and may have more credibility than an in-house system. However, it may mean entering into competition or collaboration with software houses.

5.7 Conclusions

This chapter set out to examine future developments of expert systems for the profession by assessing the effects that might arise from the proliferation of such systems. It is unlikely that any serious developer will escape a share of failed systems. The pitfall of applying an inappropriate technology is as present with expert systems as with other forms of information technology (Bakos and Treacy, 1986). In view of the optimism surrounding the use of such systems, particularly by the distributors of proprietary software, there is a need to guard against a situation in which the expert system becomes a 'solution looking for a problem', and domains are scoured accordingly until such a 'problem' is found. The circumstances that produce a successful system in a technical or scientific domain are not necessarily likely to produce the same results in a commercial or business domain. There is undoubtedly scope for systems operating at a low level of expertise, as suggested by Dreyfus and Dreyfus (1986) and others. Such systems may well be of the 'quick and dirty' variety, but they are no less successful because of that. There undoubtedly exists a niche in the accounting profession for expert system applications, particularly small systems. Other domains are already indicating that the lessons learned from the construction of small systems will not necessarily be transferable to large systems (Connell 1988), and most accountanting firms are unlikey to adopt a pioneering role in addressing these problems.

Perhaps one of the greatest benefits of expert systems, which may prove in the future to be their most successful feature, is the insight gained into what constitutes 'knowledge' or 'expertise' in a particular domain during the construction of such systems. Through building the system, the organisation becomes aware of those skills and tasks which are important in the successful conduct of its business. This can prove invaluable during recruitment and training, for example. The expert can learn during the knowledge elicitation process exactly how she applies and makes use of her expertise in solving problems. This reflective activity most typically takes place during knowledge acquisition, but may re-occur during system testing, and possibly even consultation. Extremely valuable insights into the decision process may be gained both by the knowledge engineer and the expert. Thus the process of building the system may become more valuable than the system itself. Some accounting systems have even been developed with this aim in mind (Steinbart 1986). However, the problem of attaching financial value to this process of reflection may lead to exaggerated claims similar to those made for some management information systems a decade ago, with similar consequences.

PART TWO

A Case Study

This second part of the book focuses upon the process of producing an expert system prototype. Chapter 6 reviews the methodological issues associated with the production of an expert system as software; Chapter 7 provides the background to the case study and the chosen application domain; Chapter 8 gives a detailed account of the development of an expert system prototype and indicate to an erstwhile expert system builder some of the pitfalls and characteristics of the process involved. Chapter 9 describes in detail the operational characteristics of the prototype constructed, and indicates some ways in which this prototype could be developed into a much larger system. This example will, we hope, provide the reader with an opportunity to compare how the system's expertise might be matched with that of a human expert. Chapter 10 compares the tools used during the construction process. Finally, Chapter 11 draws together and reinforces the lessons learned from the construction exercise by highlighting the scope and depth of expertise which can, and cannot, be represented adequately by an expert system.

Chapter 6

Developing an Expert System

6.1 Managing the Software Development

Since expert systems constitute a class of software it would seem appropriate to think in terms of planning their construction from a software engineering viewpoint. This chapter summarises how a conventional software project is often run, explains in what essentials expert systems differ from conventional systems, and offers some preliminary conclusions as to how an expert system project ought to be conducted.

6.1.1 Conventional software system development

The lifecycle of a conventional software project typically begins with the articulation of a problem followed by a feasibility study to determine if a solution to the problem exists and whether the solution is available at an acceptable cost and in an acceptable timescale.

The next phase involves specifying the system from the viewpoint of the user, detailing the system's inputs, outputs, functions and integration requirements. The resulting document is called a functional specification. Then a system specification is written which describes how the requirements of the functional specification will be achieved using a computer. Next, computer programs are specified, the resulting documents describing how the system specification is executed. Ultimately, these program specifications are used by programmers who produce programs written in, for example, COBOL or FORTRAN.

Subsequently there are several levels of testing designed to satisfy the programmers, system designers, contractor and client that the software works. The client then takes delivery of the software and a period of maintenance begins (see Figure 6.1).

Changes to the developing system due to oversights and errors are managed by a set of change control procedures. Although a vital aspect of software project management, change control is often viewed as a necessary evil grafted onto the main development sequence, which ideally would be an undisturbed linear process. This attitude towards change control is one of the main differences between the life-cycles of conventional versus expert systems.

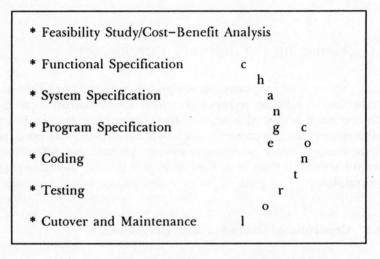

Figure 6.1 Conventional software production.

6.1.2 How expert systems differ from conventional systems

Both expert systems and conventional software projects need planning and control standards, estimates and recognisable milestones, testing procedures and standards, and appropriate documentation control. However, expert systems projects are also often characterised by:

• a lack of client familiarity with the new technology,
• the absence of a complete specification of the problem,
• the peculiar difficulties of knowledge elicitation,
• the special requirements of the user interface,
• the need for prototyping and the inevitability of re-prototyping,
• the much closer degree of client–designer cooperation throughout all phases of the project, and

• the fact that an expert system can never be considered to be finished.

These considerations have at least four major implications for the expert system development process. First, a thorough assessment of the proposed application is required at the outset. This is rather akin to an *implementation risk analysis* of the kind described by Alter (1980). Second, having decided to proceed with the project, progress is made via an iterative prototyping process during which a well-defined portion of the system is implemented in an evolutionary fashion. Third, the above process involves a great deal of *knowledge acquisition* during which a *knowledge engineer* gathers facts, information and knowledge from a variety of sources, including a human expert or experts. Finally, due consideration must be given to how to test the final product — an issue that is still largely unresolved.

When people speak of developing an expert system they often mean developing a knowledge base (that part of the system in which the domain knowledge is represented), having decided to use the inference engine that comes with a particular expert system shell (the inference engine being the part of the system that handles the control and inferential aspects of its function). As a starting point for expert systems development, the use of such shells has much to recommend it. In this case, what is being developed is data for an inference engine, not third-generation computer software, and the resulting life cycle must also reflect this fact.

6.1.3 Assessing a proposed expert system application

Any software development project must include, as one of its initial phases, a feasibility study. This has been established as standard practice for conventional computer systems for many years. A lack of sufficient consideration for the practical feasibility of what, on the surface, might appear to be a good idea, will always stand a good chance of leading to false starts, costly errors, and a general and unfortunate waste of resources and time. If this is true of conventional software systems it is even more crucial for expert systems since the latter represent a relatively new and untried paradigm in software engineering. However, the question that arises here is, 'What exactly constitutes a feasibility study for a proposed expert system?'. Proposals for conventional systems (for which nearly complete specifications can be written at the outset) may be subject to fairly complete technical, operational and financial feasibility studies. In contrast, because it is rarely possible to specify an expert system to any degree of completeness at the outset, feasibility studies of the same degree of completeness as for conventional systems are rarely possible.

Even before embarking on the construction of a prototype there is a need to justify this decision. Fortunately, although expert systems are still relatively novel in commercial environments there is nevertheless an emerging and strong consensus concerning the set of criteria that a proposed expert system application should be subjected to before the commitment of further resources to its development. The consideration of these criteria forms the basis of the first part of the feasibility study associated with a proposed application. The most important of these criteria are now presented (Prerau 1985).

The criteria are grouped according to whether they are most concerned with management, users, the task being addressed, or the expert who will be debriefed of his or her expertise.

Management
(a) the project should have strong managerial support,
(b) domain area managers should have previously identified the need for the system,
(c) introduction of the system should not be politically sensitive,
(d) the knowledge involved should not be politically sensitive.

Users
(e) the users should have realistic expectations,
(f) the task should have been agreed upon by systems developers and users,
(g) the user group should be cooperative and patient.

Task
(h) the task should constitute a well-defined objective for the system,
(i) the task domain should be characterised by the use of expertise, judgement, experience and heuristics,
(j) algorithmic approaches to the task should be inappropriate
(k) the task should require primarily symbolic reasoning,
(l) the task domain should be well bounded,
(m) the system should require development or research, but not both,
(n) the task should be moderately difficult,
(o) the task should be narrow and self-contained,
(p) the task domain should be fairly stable.

Expert
(q) recognised experts solve the problem today,
(r) the expertise required is not available on a reliable and continuing basis,
(s) an expert for the project exists,
(t) the expert has a good reputation
(u) the expert has accumulated expertise over a number of years,
(v) the expert will commit a substantial amount of time to the project,
(w) the expert is articulate, cooperative and personable.

6.1.4 The expert system life cycle (prototyping)

The general view of an expert system life cycle is that it consists of two phases, a prototype phase and a target system phase. A 'prototype' is a system that demonstrates the full functionality of the target system but which addresses a small though representative part of the proposed application domain. There are several good reasons why expert systems development should begin with the development of a prototype. First, it constitutes a feasibility exercise for the development of the target system: if it turns out that it is not possible to develop the desired functionality using an expert systems approach then not much would have been lost through an attempt at building a small prototype. Second, it is a means of uncovering the nature of the problem: because one is working with knowledge rather than data, it is not possible to completely specify a system ahead of coding since too little is yet known about the problem being addressed. Prototyping is essentially a mandatory exercise in incremental design, progress being made by exploration, informed guesswork, and learning from early mistakes. Third, prototyping offers an attractive way of determining time and resource estimates for the final product. The prototyping process may also include the development of documentation such as functional, system and user interface specifications. However, the degree to which these documents are developed grows as the iterative cycle is repeated — they are not written once and for all ahead of coding as for a conventional system (although, it should be said, that prototyping is increasingly being used in the development of conventional systems).

Initially, a sub-domain for prototyping must be chosen. Ideally, this will enable the prototype to address the whole range of functionality anticipated of the target system. It should also be clear at this stage who the user of the system will be and at what level the expertise will be pitched.

Initial decisions with respect to development hardware and software must be taken here as well initial decisions about which knowledge representation scheme and control structure to use. The decisions taken at this stage are not hard-and-fast. They should be reconsidered in the light of later experience when more appropriate judgements may be made.

The focus of prototyping is an iterative knowledge elicitation process during which a 'knowledge engineer' elicits appropriate information from an expert in the domain being modelled. This knowledge is represented using an appropriate scheme and added to an ever-growing knowledge base. During this process, as a result of the expert inspecting early software expressions of his expertise, the desired functionality of the system is identified and documented. For monitoring purposes a user community, a group of potential users of the final system, is established. The function of such a group is to experiment with and comment on the prototype as it develops, and to feed back commentary to the knowledge engineer as frequently as is practicable. 'Change control' is therefore seen as an integral and integrated part of the expert systems development life-cycle.

At the end of each iteration the design team may take one of four decisions: it may decide to begin another iteration; it may decide that the prototype is good enough and so continue on to the target system phase; it may decide that the approach being used is unlikely to produce a solution to the problem and a new one begun; or it may decide to abandon the whole exercise.

This proposed life cycle for expert system development is shown in Figure 6.2. The target system phase is similar in many ways to the prototype phase except that the decisions taken with respect to the representation scheme, control structure and appropriate hardware/software are final. There remains a strong iterative element around the process of knowledge elicitation as in the prototype phase.

6.1.5 Knowledge acquisition

Knowledge acquisition, the process of acquiring the knowledge that is to be encompassed in an expert system, has been described by Feigenbaum as being the 'bottleneck' of expert systems development. To date there is no well established methodology for performing this task. The methods used by expert system developers tend to be *ad hoc*, although there is a growing amount of basic research in this area. Some of the approaches that have been used include the following:

PROTOTYPE PHASE
    Induction
    Feasibility
    Functional specification
        Choose prototype sub-domain
    System specification
        Choose:
                Representation scheme
                Control structure
                Hardware/software
        for prototype development
    Build prototype:
        Knowledge acquisition
        Knowledge representation
        Knowledge base enhancement
        User interface enhancement
        Testing:
                Validation
                Verification
    Evaluation

TARGET SYSTEM PHASE
    Prototyping + Feasibility
        Choose run-time hardware/software
        Cost-benefit analysis
        Estimates and schedules
    Functional specification
    System specification
        Choose:
                Final representation scheme
                Overall knowledge base design
                Hardware/software
    Build target system:
        Knowledge acquisition
        Knowledge representation
        Knowledge base enhancement
        User interface enhancement
        Testing:
                Validation
                Verification
    Evaluation

    Acceptance testing
    User testing
    Cutover and maintenance

Figure 6.2 An expert system construction life cycle

(a) textbooks and manuals
(b) interviews
(c) case study analysis
(d) observation
(e) protocol analysis

(a) Textbooks and manuals. Expert system builders have frequently reported that the source of information for a knowledge base was derived from existing documentation. It may be argued (especially from the cognitive emulation viewpoint) that although the result may well be useful as a system it could not be described as an expert system since the acquisition of the knowledge was not mediated by interaction with a human expert. Often, the use of existing documentation is only a preliminary stage before the expert becomes involved in the project. It is quite reasonable to build an initial prototype using reference manuals before presenting it to a busy expert who can then constructively criticise a faulty model rather than deliver his knowledge whole and uncued to the knowledge engineer. Such initial documentation-based efforts can act as foci for exception reporting by the expert. Alternatively, it may well be that the function of the identified expert task is a front end to the interpretation of masses of documented knowledge. In this case it is to be expected that most of the knowledge base will be derived from existing hardcopy and that this will be overlaid by expertise derived from an expert.

(b) Interviews. Interviewing the expert is the most commonly used method of knowledge acquisition. It requires considerable skill on the part of the knowledge engineer to be able to identify the questions that are most likely to elicit the kind of knowledge that is required. One of the problems with interviews is that the expert is generally attempting to articulate how he performed a task after the event, and that under these circumstances there is uncertainty as to the degree to which he introduces rationalisation. Another problem is that the expert is likely to digress unless the interviewer keeps his questions very specific.

(c) Case Study Analysis. One method of restraining digression by the expert is through the use of case studies. The value of presenting specific cases derives from the fact that it is much easier for a person to recall knowledge that has been cued than uncued. However, this approach still suffers from the danger of rationalisation on the part of the expert.

(d) Observation. Direct observation of the expert may take place in the purely physical sense, for example, if the expertise involves the manipulation of the controls in a processing plant, or it may be considered in the sense of an expert articulating his thoughts as he is solving a problem, for example via a fresh case study. In the latter case a tape-recording of the is transcribed and the result submitted to protocol analysis.

(e) Protocol Analysis. The idea behind protocol analysis is the assumption that there is a strong correlation between the thoughts an expert experiences as he solves a problem and the protocols that he generates as he attempts to articulate those thoughts. A great deal of research is currently underway in this area, and there is still a great deal of argument as to whether articulated protocols are valid as data for the encryption of knowledge.

6.1.6 Testing

There are three ways in which an expert system as software requires testing. First, it must be tested at the same level that conventional software is tested, that is, at the level of its third generation code (e.g. PASCAL or C). Following this it must be tested for logical consistency, that is, it must be validated. Third, it must be tested for its performance compared to human beings, that is, it must be verified.

If a shell is being used the lowest level of testing should already have been completed by the software manufacturer. The code constituting the inference engine and the user interface should already have undergone exhaustive and systematic conventional tests. A user may nevertheless come across 'bugs' in shell software and when this happens the problem is treated in the same way as a conventional software problem.

The term 'testing' when used in the context of an expert system usually refers to what has been described above as validation and verification. Again, in a well-designed inference engine validation should not be a problem and it should not be possible for a user to construct a knowledge base in which the affirmation of an assertion can lead to its own denial (e.g. A => B => C => NOT A). It should also not be possible to build structures that depend on circular reasoning (e.g. A => B => C => A). However, with the generation of products currently on the market it is often possible to include such structures and this leads, not surprisingly, to the software behaving in a strange way, even though it does not 'crash' in the conventional sense.

The interesting aspect of testing expert systems lies in verification concerned with the comparison of the performance of an expert system with that of a human expert. The two main objectives of verification correspond to whether the original motive for building the system came from a desire to produce a high-performance problem solver or a cognitive emulator. In the first instance the emphasis is on the outcome generated by the system, that is, on whether it produces an improvement on human performance. In the second instance the researcher is more concerned to discover whether the system reasons in the same way as a human expert.

One common method of verifying an expert system involves giving a batch of case studies to the system and also to a group of human experts, and then presenting the set of assessments generated, in a blind fashion, to a second group of human experts who then 'mark' the assessments. The resulting marks then form a basis upon which to judge the performance of the expert system. The resulting comparison may be expressed directly in terms of the level of performance or in terms of the correlation between the system's assessments and those of the humans.

Some researchers (see Section 4.1) have adopted refined approaches based upon protocol analysis designed to generate detailed information about how expert systems and human experts come to their judgements. This kind of work relies upon detailed comparisons made between system and human on how much time each spends in particular cognitive modes and the sequence in which these episodes occur.

Research work in the area of expert system verification is still in its infancy and is likely to remain so for some time.

6.2   Documenting a Shell-Based Expert System

The need for detailed documentation at several levels of specification is now well established for conventional software systems. There is, however, considerable debate about how to approach this task for expert systems. There are two extreme points of view. There are those who insist that expert systems should be specified to the same degree as conventional systems and there are others who maintain that it is not necessary to document an expert system at all since it should be self documenting. There are weaknesses in both these positions. In the first place it is hard to see how a system can be fully specified before full knowledge about its user requirements or its structure is known, and in the second place, although it is possible to imagine a system which is completely self-documenting, current evidence indicates that software of sufficient quality is not yet available to achieve this.

The questions that are posed in this section are 'to what degree is the conventional specification approach appropriate to an expert system implemented using a shell?' and 'if it is not appropriate then what might be?'.

To begin with, it is necessary to be clear about exactly what is being specified. Conventional software is written in 'procedural' languages such as FORTRAN, COBOL or PASCAL, which are characterised by statements detailing sequences of operations or procedures to be executed on data. The lowest level of specification is concerned with the functions that are addressed by computer programs written in these languages. However, when using an expert system shell the knowledge base is written in code which constitutes data for the shell's inference engine, which is itself written in a procedural language. The language used to code the knowledge base is generally of a 'declarative' variety. A declarative language is able to express statements about the relationships between concepts without concern for how that knowledge is to be manipulated. The procedures used for the manipulation of the declarative code are contained within the inference engine which may be considered as a black box. Thus for an expert system the specification task is centred around a body of declarative knowledge, the details of the manipulation of which have already been taken care of.

It is appropriate here to review how the specification task is typically done for a conventional system and then decide upon the appropriateness of that approach for the specification of a shell-based expert system.

6.2.1 The conventional approach

Before a line of code is written a conventional software system is typically specified at three levels: functional specification, system specification, and program specification.

The *functional specification* is a document which defines, for the intended users of a proposed system, the facilities the system will offer, and what the user will have to do in order to make use of it. It thus provides a statement of the objectives that the system's designers have to meet.

The production of the functional specification is the essential first stage in the design of any conventional software system. The feasibility study, which will have preceded it, will have been concerned with the exploration of alternative solutions to a problem and will have described a recommended system, but will not have defined it. It is the functional specification that defines the functions of the system. It must be written for the proposed system's users: that is, for managers and members of the organisations and departments who will operate, supply inputs for, and/or benefit from the system, or be responsible for its auditing and/or control. The functional specification is:

(a) the basis for development of the system specification,
(b) the only place where the system's functions are expressed in a common language understandable by both the users and the system designers,
(c) the basis from which all system changes and corrections are negotiated;
(d) the basis from which acceptance tests are developed.

The *system specification* describes and details the operational design of the complete system. The elements of the system, what it will process, and how and when it will do so, are fully detailed within this document.

The system specification is written for those responsible for the design, development, testing, implementation and maintenance of the system. It is not normally written for those who will either run or use the system, although the system designers must at all times bear in mind the twin objectives of designing a system that is both runnable and usable.

The system specification forms a precise definition of how the system is to be constructed. It must correspond exactly with the contents of the functional specification since it is a specification of the manner in which the requirements of the functional specification are to be achieved.

This specification is taken as a starting point, and the system is sub-divided into logically self-contained units which address distinct functional objectives, for example, updating a file. The detailed descriptions of these operating units are called *program specifications*. A program specification is therefore a computer-oriented description of a component of the system which communicates with other components only through 'messages' and/or external files.

6.2.2 Shell-based expert systems documentation requirements

The three levels of specification for conventional systems are now considered for their appropriateness in the specification of shell-based expert systems.

The functional specification

The stated objectives of the functional specification for conventional software can be summarised as addressing the issues of user facilities and *modus operandi*. Also implicit in the discussion are the issues of the overall function of the system and the identification of the user. There seems to be no reason why such a document should not be appropriate as an evolving part of the specification of a shell-based expert system.

The system specification

In the context of shell-based expert systems there would appear to be no need for a system specification as conventionally defined. The area addressed by this level of specification is divided between the inference engine of the expert system shell and the knowledge base. In as much as the inference engine comes packaged and fully developed with the shell, no additional specification work for it should be necessary. The knowledge base usually conforms to a high-level-declarative syntax and constitutes data for the inference engine. As data it can hardly be considered worthy of a system specification. However, it may be argued that there should be a document in which the knowledge to be encapsulated by the expert system should be recorded in an *implementation-independent* fashion. Such a document might be called The knowledge base specification. This document would contain all the knowledge/information/heuristics derived from the expert during the knowledge elicitation process expressed in an appropriate 'pseudo-code'. Such a document would not be necessary if the tool being used were sufficiently expressive (see below).

The program specification

There is no need for a program specification in the conventional sense if there is no requirement for a conventional system specification. Although the knowledge base constitutes part of the area that would conventionally be addressed by a system specification, when the knowledge base is considered in the context of the corresponding program specification it would appear that no distinction can be made between the system specification and the program specification expressions of the knowledge base. This assumes that program specifications are logical, implementation-independent statements. If program specifications are considered to be implementation-dependent then no distinction can be made between them and the code derived from them. Therefore there is nothing to be added by having a program specification level for shell-based expert systems since all the information required is either in the knowledge base specification or in the knowledge base code itself.

6.2.3 Can a knowledge base be truly self-documenting?

At the outset it should be recognised that what is being developed is data for an inference engine and also that parallels can be drawn with the development of, say, COBOL code that could be considered as data for a compiler.

For a knowledge base to be self-documenting the software tool used (be it a shell or a tool-kit) must be sufficiently expressive to allow a relatively non-technical reader to gather a sufficient degree of meaning from the software listing. This also means that the listing should be fairly free of implementation-dependent terms, i.e. it should be free of jargon that is specific to the tool used. More fundamentally, it means that the language used to express the expertise in the system is likely to correspond more to a specification (i.e. declarative) medium than one with many procedural elements. This will have implications for the structure of the knowledge base. In particular it leads to the guideline that the knowledge base should be structured so that procedural knowledge is separated from declarative knowledge. This separation is performed to a very large degree by having the inference engine separate from the knowledge base. It could be taken that the degree to which procedural code is necessary in the knowledge base is a measure of the degree to which the inference engine is lacking.

The problem with the above, even given that the tool used has the required degree of expressiveness, is that the level at which the documentation is produced is at the level of the specification (i.e. declaration) of the knowledge. This would correspond more to the system specification level of a conventional system than, say, the functional specification level.

Viewing the prototyping process as an exercise in problem structure development and discovery it is likely that an appropriate approach would be to rely solely upon system auto-documentation until the prototype has been deemed 'finished', but then to write a higher-level 'functional specification' that would give an overview of the structure of the knowledge base and the system facilities, which, at this time would be relatively stable.

Chapter 7

The Application Domain

7.1   Background

It was decided at the outset of this study that

(a)   the software to be used would be chosen from the range of expert system shells already available on the market, in other words, that no special-purpose software would be written using a lower-level approach,

(b)   more than one expert would contribute to the project, and

(c)   the area of investigation would be the assessment of business risks associated with computer installations.

The reasoning behind these initial decisions lay in the context in which the project was set up. First, the resources available to the project were limited to about two man-years so there was no question of using other than expert system shells as the software development medium. Second, since the funding body (the ICAEW) caters to the accounting community at large it was concerned that more than one member of that community be represented in it. In a sense, the project could be said to have followed the pattern of a 'community club' performing 'pre-competitive' research, the fruits of which would be disseminated throughout the club's membership. Third, the procedure for determining the location of the study required a choice of application area prior to beginning the study, considering the interests of Institute members, available expertise and other research in this area, without the benefit of a feasibility study.

These initial decisions, and especially the second two, had important implications for the progress of the study as a whole.

The case study was mainly concerned with the knowledge elicitation process, rather than with system implementation issues that would occur during a later stage of the project. In what follows the strategies for eliciting the knowledge from two computer audit managers are described in some detail, 'warts and all', in order to give the reader a flavour of the kinds of events that can occur in such situations. As the narrative proceeds lessons and guidelines are drawn out and considered as heuristics in their own right for the task of knowledge elicitation.

7.2 The Chosen Application Domain

The problem domain chosen for the expert system was the assessment of business risks associated with computer installations. This section briefly surveys this area. The general nature of some of the risks are described as well as the kinds of controls that may be used to manage them. Finally, a view is presented of the reviewer in the context of his task.

Computer systems are becoming ubiquitous in the commercial and industrial world and are already used for the automated execution of many of the transactions hitherto performed manually. Accounts, previously kept in paper files, now increasingly claim magnetic tape or disks as their main home. This movement from paper-to silicon-based systems as the principal means of information storage, manipulation and transfer has necessitated an appropriate degree of growth and adaptation in auditing procedures, and the use of computer systems as a tool in the management of business has brought with it new problems and new risks. The growing awareness of these new categories of business risk has been accompanied by the evolution of a corresponding species of expert. It is the expertise exhibited by this kind of expert that was the focus for this study.

7.2.1 Classes of computer systems business risk

Computer systems business risks may be classified into five groups: development risks, errors, business interruption, unauthorised access to information, and fraud.

Development risks include those due to:
• not developing or planning new systems,

- developing inappropriate systems,
- delays in systems implementation,
- insufficient attention to:
    long-term planning,
    feasibility studies,
    proper systems specifications,
    hardware/software selection,
    project control,
- security/control requirements not being integrated into the design process.

Errors may be due to faults in:
- data entry,
- software developments/amendments,
- execution of routine housekeeping procedures,
- the use of special utilities,
- customisation of standard packages.

Business interruption could be caused by:
- software failure,
- hardware failure,
- software or data destruction due to fire, flood or malicious damage.

Unauthorised access to information could occur through:
- normal terminal enquiry facilities,
- the use of special programs to read data files,
- the physical removal of files or printouts,
- the tapping of telecommunication lines.

Fraud could occur through such occurrences as:
- unauthorised amendment of payment instructions prior to entry,
- direct entry of unauthorised transactions,
- unauthorised change to programs,
- use of special programs to make unauthorised changes to data,
- removal and amendment of computer files before replacement,
- introduction or interception of transactions via telecommunication networks.

7.2.2   Classes of controls

By and large, two types of direct control may be used to manage the above risks: preventive controls and detective controls.

Preventive controls are designed to prevent threatening events. Examples include:

- data input controls,
- security devices to prevent unauthorised access to equipment,
- passwords,
- telecommunications message authentication,
- system specification controls,
- testing controls,
- documentation controls.

Detective controls are designed to detect and contain events that bypass preventive controls. For example:

- fire detection and extinguishing equipment,
- redundancy in telecommunication and computer networks as protection against individual component breakdown,
- contingency recovery plans in case of fire, flood, explosion,
- exception reports.

7.2.3 Assessment of risk: the reviewer's task

The job of a reviewer, when faced with the task of inspecting the computer activities within a business, is to identify potential risks, to assess the effectiveness of the controls designed to manage those risks, and to advise how control may be improved. The reviewer carries with him not only a general view of his objective and knowledge of its structure but also specific knowledge relevant to the particulars of the client for which the review is being performed. Thus the reviewer will know not only which control objectives he or she is interested in but also how those control objectives may be affected by the particular organisational structure of the client company and by the particular hardware and software being used. It is this function that is being addressed here.

Chapter 8

The Knowledge Elicitation Experience

8.1 Introduction

Knowledge elicitation is often said to be the 'bottleneck' in the design of expert systems. The reasons for this are various:

(a) Experts are a scarce resource and their time is expensive; thus a firm may hesitate to release an expert because of the cost and an expert may hesitate to cooperate for fear of making himself redundant.

(b) Assuming that an expert is willing to cooperate, it is also important that he be reasonably articulate because the medium of knowledge transfer will be largely verbal.

(c) Even given a willing and articulate expert, success is not guaranteed because he might not be aware of much of the knowledge that he uses routinely but unconsciously during the course of his professional duties.

(d) Even in a single application domain the knowledge being sought may take a variety of forms each requiring its own appropriate method of elicitation. The knowledge engineer performing the elicitation task needs techniques for first uncovering the overall structure of the knowledge, and then eliciting the different kinds of knowledge that the expert possesses. Such techniques are still in the early stages of development.

Knowledge elicitation is one of the phases of the iterative process associated with the design of an expert system prototype. It feeds into the other phases and is itself influenced by them. In particular there is a strong interaction between knowledge elicitation and knowledge representation. This should not be surprising since in order for the knowledge to be recorded on paper some preliminary decisions have to be taken about the structures in which it might be conveniently expressed.

This chapter presents an account of the knowledge elicitation process as experienced in the case study. The account takes the form of a narrative describing the events as they happened. An attempt is made to trace parallel developments in the elicitation process, together with their impact on the developing model in the application domain, although the emphasis is on the nature of the events occurring during the interview process.

The work covers the interaction with one expert over fifteen knowledge elicitation sessions and with a second expert over a further thirteen sessions.

8.2   The First Expert

Preliminary meeting
The story begins on the premises of a major accounting firm that had expressed interest in participating in the project. An initial meeting was arranged at which the author was introduced to the expert and at which the application sub-domain for the prototype and the users of the final system were discussed.

System function identification
It was decided that the application sub-domain should be the general controls (i.e. the non-processing controls) associated with a computer installation. The main function identified was that of a 'troubleshooter' sufficiently generally expert to be able to identify which areas of a computer system should be subject to closer scrutiny by a computer audit specialist.

User identification
It was envisaged that there would be four classes of user:

(a)   The relatively DP-naive chartered accountant working in industry.
(b)   The small audit firm, not employing specialists, that is worried about not doing proper audits for its clients.
(c)   The more sophisticated external auditor who would use the system to build a more extensive approach – a more detailed trouble-shooter.

(d) The internal audit department which would use the system to assess the risk level of aspects of the computer system under scrutiny with a view to establishing a way of directing audit resources to the riskiest areas.

Establishment of the working context
The envisaged pattern of the knowledge elicitation sessions was as follows:

(a) The interviews would be about two hours long.
(b) They would be tape-recorded and transcribed as necessary.
(c) The evolving model would be expressed using a proprietary expert system shell and demonstrated to the expert for comment as appropriate.

At this point the only readily available shell was SAVOIR. As comparative evaluation of shells was part of the study objective, and since nothing was known about the structure of the problem being addressed, SAVOIR became the default software choice.

The interviews (first expert)

There follows a summary of the kinds of events that occurred during the interviews with the first expert.

INTERVIEW No. 1.1
The expert was invited to speak generally about his task. What followed was largely monologue during which the expert gave a description of his working environment and function — an overview of the domain. Some structure began to emerge even at this early stage. For example, it was established that there were different kinds of review objective, i.e. audit, consultancy, etc. Also, a sampling of the kinds of event that could occur during task execution were described: for example, the necessity of deciding whether to perform compliance or substantive testing.

With some encouragement, the expert then began to talk in more specific terms, for example, he explored the nature of non-processing (i.e. general) controls.

Some of the firm's information gathering documentation (a summary checklist) was produced and discussed and the function of this documentation in the review process was explored as were the disadvantages of an uninformed checklist approach. This led to a discussion of the expert's mode of operation which in turn led to a discussion of the proposed expert system's mode of operation and form of advice.

INTERVIEW No. 1.2

At the beginning of this session a software representation of the material covered so far was shown to the expert. The demonstration was very limited, mainly serving to familiarise the expert with the appearance of the shell's user interface.

The aim of the interview, to obtain a firmer view of the overall structure, perhaps informed by a case study analysis, was then discussed. Aids used during the process of knowledge elicitation, including inference nets, clarification questions and systems documentation, were considered. 'Clarification' questions arising from the previous interview were aired.

The expert was then invited to talk through a case study. He introduced the case study with some preamble about his audit approach. He then talked his way through the case study notes describing particular points and problems. During this process he frequently provided more general information about both his and his firm's audit approach. This was found to be useful. It transpired that the expert knew almost without thinking which of the questions on the summary checklist were applicable in any particular case. The possibility of the project having access to the firm's detailed but company confidential checklist was raised. It was felt that such a list would form the basis of a much better focused interview. Access to this checklist rested upon authorisation by the expert's supervisor.

INTERVIEW No. 1.3

At about this time a crude paper representation of the domain began to evolve. The author would bring the paper model to an interview and the expert would amend it, usually quite radically. Indeed, for the first few weeks this model showed no sign of becoming stable (see Figure 8.1 for a typical example)

The issue of company profile was addressed. The question asked here was 'Could you identify how the characteristics of the company can be used as a guide to determine which of the firm's checklist questions should be considered?'. In response the expert produced such concepts as financial vs non-financial, size, complexity of the computer installation, risk category, etc. The idea of an 'acceptable control profile' as a function of company characteristics arose for the first time. The importance of review objective was also men-

tioned in passing. A general discussion followed about the reliability
of information sources and its effect in various types of business.

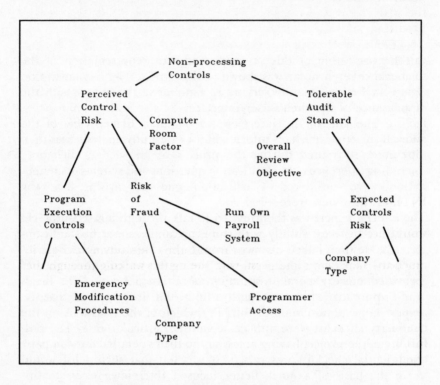

Figure 8.1 An early domain model.

The summary checklist was used as a focus for discussion. The
intention here was that for each question on the summary checklist
the expert would be asked 'in what kind of organisation would you
ask this question?', 'why are you asking the question?' and 'what are
the consequences if the answer is no?'.

After some deliberation the expert expressed frustrated dis-
satisfaction with the questions on the summary checklist saying that
they were arbitrary and did not reflect the way in which he worked.
He then took those questions he considered useful and expounded
on the context in which they were used.

INTERVIEW No. 1.4

The latest paper representation was inspected it having been found that single-page diagrams were a very useful device for focusing on the structure of the knowledge being uncovered. The most recently produced software mock-up was inspected.

The case study was repeated in more detail while referring to the paper model produced after the previous interview in order to check whether the model corresponded to the expert's description. Again, the discussion covered much general material in the course of analysing the particulars of the case study. The author still got the feeling that an appropriately low level of material was not being addressed and that there was a lack of low-level focus. This case study took about two and a half hours to talk through.

INTERVIEW No. 1.5

The expert reported that regretfully the firm's confidential checklist would not be made available to the project.

A second case study was introduced; this seemed to go in much the same way as the first, with the expert walking through the review reflecting on the information-gathering process.

After this session it was clear that the time had come for a review of progress to date; it was felt that the objectives of the exercise were not sufficiently well defined and that in order to progress further a close examination of what had thus far transpired was crucial.

Preparation for the review

The focus for the review was a group of five questioning statements suggesting at what stage the modelling process might be, and some further but preliminary commentary on them. These issues and the corresponding commentary were brought to the expert's attention at the following meeting.

The statements

How were we doing? After five knowledge elicitation interviews we still had not arrived at a demonstrable mock-up, although the inference net generated as a result of the elicitation process was easily incorporated in a SAVOIR program. Several possibilities suggested themselves:

(1) We were suffering from a lack of direction with respect to various aspects of the system specification and in particular with respect to the effect on this of the choice of user and user interface (i.e. the *modus operandi*). Thus, 'Who *exactly* is the intended user?' and 'What *exactly* is the envisaged mode of operation?'.

(2) The conceptual level addressed was too high. In other words, we had not yet narrowed the application domain far enough. Relevant questions here were, 'How do you know when you are at the right conceptual level?' and 'If the conceptual level is too high how do you refine it down?'.

(3) We were doing fine — but nobody said it would be easy. The conceptual level addressed corresponded to that of the expert but there was a need to look at the nature of the links joining the objects. The questions here were, 'What kinds of links have been used in other systems and are they relevant to our case?' and 'Does this have any repercussions on the most appropriate knowledge representation scheme, and in particular what does it say with regard to the particular software being used?'.

(4) The nature of the expertise involved had received insufficient consideration. Thus, 'What is the nature of the expert's expertise?', 'Why have the methods used so far failed to elicit it?', 'Is there an alternative model of the expert's knowledge that could lead us to other methods of knowledge elicitation?'.

(5) Knowledge elicitation was obviously very inefficient. 'Is there any better way such as induction? Could an expert do it himself for other than a simple system?'.

Commentary

(1)   *User and user interface definition*
During the initial meeting four kinds of user were described, and it was assumed that the same system would be appropriate for all classes of user. Was this assumption justified? Are not the objectives of an internal audit department worried about resource management different from those of a relatively DP-naive chartered accountant working in industry? The user interface involved would almost certainly have to be very different in these cases.

It was evidently necessary to decide upon one narrowly defined class of user, preferably the one requiring the least sophisticated user interface. Having decided upon the user class, case studies could be run through with this user always in mind in an attempt to get a feel for the level of dialogue that would be generated by the user interface.

(2) *The conceptual level*

Using Prerau's (1985) checklist it seemed useful to consider some of his guidelines relevant for the identification of a problem suitable for an expert system's application and apply them to our case.

Problem types:

T1 The task should not require knowledge from a very large number of areas.

T2 The task should be clearly defined. At the project outset, there should be a precise definition of the inputs and outputs of the system to be developed.

Problem bounds:

B1 The task should neither be too easy (taking a human expert less than a few minutes) nor too difficult (requiring more than a few hours for an expert).

B2 The task should be sufficiently narrow and self-contained. The aim is not for a system that is expert in an entire domain, but for a system that is an expert in a limited task within the domain.

T1 urges focus on the domain scope, T2 on the domain function, B1 on the general level of complexity and B2 on the degree of independence.

Thus we should ask whether the scope of our application is sufficiently narrow, its function sufficiently clear, its general level of complexity appropriate, and its universe of discourse relatively self-contained.

In order to provide some kind of metric with which to gauge the conceptual level addressed in the proposed system it seemed useful to examine examples of rules taken from other expert systems (e.g. MYCIN, DIPMETER ADVISOR and the ALFEX club company health assessor).

(3) *The inference method*

The question addressed here was how the value of an object could be derived as a function of its determinants. This assumed that a satisfactory range of values could been defined for each object. Some expert systems rely on assigning certainty factors or other such scalars to assertions or hypotheses in the knowledge base. The problem with this approach was that it was essentially arbitrary in those cases where the expertise being modelled was heuristic rather than probabilistic. Other approaches might be to use crisp or even fuzzy logic, although it could be argued that the latter also suffered from the drawback of the arbitrary choice of numerical representation. At this juncture it seemed appropriate simply to 'ask the expert' to see whether what he said could be represented in a linguistically clear way.

It seemed possible that a correlation existed between the choice of inference mechanism and the choice of representation method — 'asking the expert' would produce statements about both. The next difficult stage would be to decide how to attempt to implement the model given the range of available software, and also what compromises would be needed given the limitations of current technology and resources.

(4)   *The nature of the expertise*

Thus far during the knowledge elicitation interviews the author found it very difficult to bring the expert down to what was felt to be an appropriately detailed level. When telling the expert about this difficulty his response was that he was already operating at the lowest level that he used in his work. The author was suspicious about this, but assuming this was true it should have been possible to explicate the links between the objects in the inference net without the need for too much reclassification. A way forward here might be to generate a consultation dialogue by systematically working through the paper representation using one of the case studies starting at the top level goal ('the non-processing controls are good if') and working down the inference net.

Another approach which occurred to the author was as follows. The currency of the expert appeared to be 'the question'. It was noticeable that when asked to explain a point he would almost invariably and spontaneously respond by articulating the question that would be most appropriate in the client situation relevant to the point of clarification. Subsequently, when asked to explain why he would ask that question, the expert often had to reflect at length before replying.

In constructing a model by generalising from the above an auditor walks into a situation and intuitively knows which questions to ask. This is just one aspect of his expertise, the other being to know how to evaluate the answers to the questions. It is as if an auditor carries with him a very large but implicit checklist of questions from which he selects those appropriate to the particular situation in which he finds himself. Indeed, accountants are renowned for their checklists and in inspecting the latter one is forcefully struck by the intelligence (i.e. the expertise) behind their design. Therefore a more systematic, and perhaps more efficient, way to go seemed to be to collect together those checklists relevant to our domain, focus upon a particular case study and then go through the checklist asking the expert such questions as, 'in this situation, would you ask this question?', 'why?/why not?', 'if yes, what central object/concept are you interested in by asking this question?', 'how will you use the information gained?', 'what are the implications if the answer is no (or some other value)?'. This is essentially a data-driven, bottom-up approach as opposed to the goal-driven, top-down approach described in the previous paragraph.

(5)   *The inefficiency of the interview approach*
At this time it was not at all clear how else to proceed. The number of concepts being dealt with seemed to be too large to contemplate using a method such as repertory grid analysis. Induction as an approach seem infeasible because too few examples were available. Whether the expert could do it himself came down to an examination of the role of the knowledge engineer himself. For the time being it was assumed that his role was largely concerned with facilitating the expert's articulation of his knowledge, and that had the expert been alone he would likely have overlooked factors which he considered 'obvious' but which in fact warranted explicit treatment in the developing system.

INTERVIEW No. 1.6
The review discussion gave rise to the following actions and decisions:

(a)   The view of the user was narrowed down to an internal audit department which would use the system to assess the 'risk level' of aspects of the computer system under scrutiny.
(b)   In terms of user requirements it was agreed that the system could be useful to serve an internal training function, and also that the user interface needed a great deal of attention.
(c)   The conceptual level addressed was tentatively confirmed − it appeared to be of much the same order as that for the ALFEX health risk system, which seemed reasonable.
(d)   Our elicitation strategy should be a mixture of bottom-up (taking the reviewer's questions as the products of his experience and attempting to discover the processes leading to their choice) and top-down (identifying the 'goals' being addressed by the questions and attempting to set them in an hierarchical framework). The

next phase would be to investigate the evaluation of the question responses, e.g. in terms of business risk.

Our differing versions of the paper model were discussed. This was a valuable exercise; the nodes in the diagrams served as foci for the expert's thoughts. The discussion centred on the significance of such ideas as 'perceived controls risk', 'tolerable audit standard', 'overall review objective', 'DP complexity', 'expected controls risk', 'segregation of duties', 'hardware', 'software', 'fraud', etc.

It became apparent that the scope of the domain was much too large, so it was decided to narrow this down. An initial candidate for the new sub-domain was 'access controls' which are those controls, both physical and logical (i.e. mediated by software), that act to limit access to the computer and its paraphernalia. Subsequently the area of 'change control' was settled on as the new sub-domain since, in the expert's view, 'access controls' would be too narrow an area. Change control is the collection of procedures designed to ensure the orderly execution and documentation of changes to software.

The enquiry proceeded something along the lines of 'what's the next question that you ask?' and then 'why do you ask that?'. For example,

Question: How is a program change initiated?

Explanation: A program change may have been initiated for one of two reasons: either there is a bug in a program, or a user (for example) wants something different on his reports. So I tend to split that into emergency changes and routine changes.

Having decided to focus on change control the expert proceeded in much the same way as he had with respect to the much broader area of non-processing controls. However, it was clear this time that the 'granularity' of the issues being discussed was much more manageable.

The process seemed much smoother than before. A new and simplified control model emerged which seemed more powerful and stable and which seemed more suitable as a framework for a paper model (see Figure 8.2).

This model was interesting because it represented a separating out of the control knowledge of the application from the detailed domain-specific knowledge. Domain knowledge is characterised by statements of fact or opinion ('the access controls for the client's installation would be satisfactory if'), whereas control knowledge is

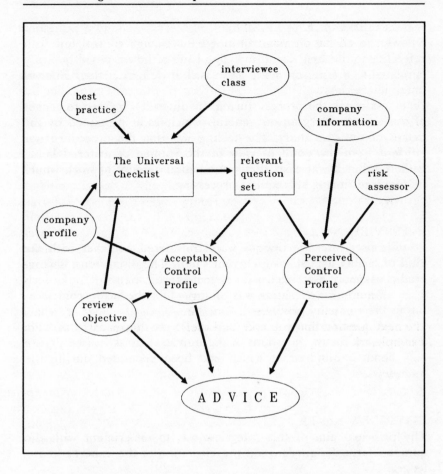

Figure 8.2 A control model for risk assessment.

characterised by actions ('to come to a conclusion about the level of risk, the acceptable quality of control must be compared with the perceived quality of control'). In other words, the control knowledge seemed to provide a framework within which the domain knowledge could be manipulated. In this context the evolving paper model became a control model. The way in which this model emerged was somewhat mysterious but seemed to be mediated by the insight afforded by a shift in focus from 'the control objective' to 'the question' in the author's perception of the domain.

INTERVIEW No. 1.7

Knowledge elicitation was continued for change control but with reference to the first case study. The issue of how a posed question is related to the person being addressed arose here — the matter of 'interviewee class'.

As usual, the process during this interview seemed to consist of the expert enlarging on general principles as prompted by the details of the case study. The feeling was that the procedure was efficient from the point of view of the volume of material being gathered, but it was clear that a substantial amount of work would be required during subsequent processing.

INTERVIEW No. 1.8

Possible user interface designs were considered, together with the kind of facility available on current shells. The discussion also covered areas more associated with system specification.

Knowledge elicitation was continued for the factors contributing to the company profile.

A question form (see Appendix D) was designed to provide a framework for the questions of the universal checklist (see Figure 8.2), about a hundred of which had been generated during the interviews.

INTERVIEW No. 1.9

The principal aim of this interview was to experiment with the question form designed to aid the elicitation of the expert's knowledge.

The session began by working through all of the questions so far collected with the idea of allotting to each a 'phase' and a 'control context'. By 'phase' was meant a procedural component of the overall activity under scrutiny (change control in this case). By 'control context' was meant the general area of purpose which the question addressed. The phases and control contexts identified were as follows:

Phases: Initiation, justification, specification, execution, testing and implementation.

Control contexts: Authorisation, preventive control and detective control (including: segregation of duties, documentation, standards, agent suitability, competence)

Here 'agent suitability' refers to the degree of match between a task and the person doing it, and 'competence' is associated with factors which give an overall idea of the client's level of competence.

It was found that a phase was sometimes 'its own' context, such as Justification, and also that more than one context could apply to the same phase. It was expected that at the more detailed level, control contexts would be decomposed into or associated with specific control objectives. From an implementation standpoint it seemed clear that a user could have the option of focusing by phase or by context, or by a combination of the two.

The motivation behind this exercise was to structure the knowledge base in a way that would facilitate a smooth dialogue with the user. At a later stage, having obtained a reasonably connected flow of questioning, the issue of how the answers to the questions were used would be addressed.

After this, a small group of questions was chosen for analysis using the drafted question form (during this session there was time to address only one question). This process served to highlight inadequacies in the form and also to provide a much better idea of how much knowledge elicitation would be required for the implementation of a full system (an enormous amount).

It was found that it was not necessary to transcribe the tapes generated since virtually all of the information gathered was well recorded on the form. It would appear that as formalisation of knowledge elicitation proceeds, there is a rapidly decreasing need for verbatim transcripts of the interviews.

INTERVIEW No. 1.10
The aim of this interview was to continue the process of knowledge elicitation via use of the question form.

The session began by reviewing the latest version of the software model that had been prepared for the meeting. The model now contained most of the features that had previously been demonstrated separately. In running what there was of the model the expert commented that as he proceeded the questions appearing on the screen stimulated him to think of many other associated issues. Again, this raised the questions of granularity and knowledge base completeness. Having limited the prototype domain to the issues surrounding non-processing controls and then to the area of change control, it was felt that we might be obliged to limit it further, perhaps to a single phase of change control and perhaps even further to a particular context.

The computer program ran very slowly. It was clear that at the current rate of growth the response time would soon become intolerable. The SAVOIR code being run was about 2200 lines long and involved only about 100 of what might be considered 'rules' in SAVOIR terms. This aspect of the project was therefore beginning to point in the direction of the evaluation of the different tools that might be chosen for the implementation of such a system.

The computer mock-up having been reviewed, the issue of the relationship between the questions and the question form was again addressed. This led, almost immediately, to a digression involving an analysis of the characteristics associated with company profile. This was because the conditions under which the change control questions would be asked were a partial function of the company profile (as indeed was predicted).

An analysis of the original list of change control questions was returned to. What transpired confirmed the experience of the previous session. The knowledge engineer and the expert were reminded of the huge amount of information that they were attempting to tap into. In the knowledge engineer's mind this confirmed Bowden's (1977) argument against the idea that expert systems 'dehumanise', but they indeed serve to remind us of the power of the human cerebral apparatus.

There was time to process only a few of the 100 questions that had been identified, but even in those that were dealt with, the process of answering them served the purpose of identifying the very low-level goals with which the reviewer was ultimately concerned. In other words, the elicitation was achieving the level of the 'why' of the reviewer's questioning process though related to a limited aspect of the application domain and in a limited context.

As an attempt to clear the way forward, the knowledge engineer identified what he thought would likely be the next steps in the elicitation process.

(1) Develop the context of the elicited questions. Generate other, related questions, extract associated control objectives, identify interviewee class influences, identify company profile influences, identify review objective influences.

(2) Analyse case studies. Construct the 'acceptable control profile' section, i.e. acceptable control profile is a function of company profile and review objective.

(3) Consider the control objectives or, rather, consider what decisions the expert makes (are these about the control objectives?) and how he reaches them (the inference mechanisms).

(4) Develop the user interface. Critique the model, test it with case studies, try it on other potential users. Ask: 'what is it like so far?', 'what questions would you like to be able to ask?', 'what kind of advice would you like to be able to get out of it?'.

INTERVIEW No. 1.11

This interview focused upon the 'implementation' phase of change control.

It was evident that the prototype domain had to be narrowed further and to this end the expert was asked how he felt about addressing any of the individual phases of 'change control' separately from the others. He said he would be fairly happy in treating the 'implementation' phase in this way. The issue of reclassification depth was also broached. The expert felt that a limit had to be set on the degree to which goals were reclassified in order to give the design process a chance to be completed through all of its aspects. In particular, he was conscious that he had not yet begun to address the way in which the expert came to his decisions and judgements, i.e. the 'inference mechanisms' that the expert used.

The emerging structure of the knowledge surrounding the elicited questions had been encapsulated in a 'question form' which was then used to inform each implementation question. The knowledge engineer generally followed two connected lines of enquiry, i.e. 'why are you asking this question?' and 'what are the risks involved if the answer is no?'. These types of questions generally enabled the identification of two kinds of 'goals': control objectives and business risks. It was thought possible that their existence would have implications for the final architecture of the system.

The expert expressed some reservations with respect to the idea of the 'context' of a question — he was not sure that this reflected the way in which he worked. However, the fact that such 'contexts' had surfaced seemed indicative of something and upon further questioning the expert suggested that he uses or might make use of the concept in the production of his final reports.

INTERVIEW No. 1.12

The aim of this interview was to investigate the inference mechanisms associated with the 'implementation' phase of change control.

First the software model was reviewed, which now incorporated the implementation phase to the extent it had been developed during the previous meeting. The knowledge engineer had prepared a set of questions about the model which were addressed. A summary of the points as they emerged follows.

(a) The overall structure of the model dialogue was reasonable although the phrasing of the questions could be improved.

(b) The relevant question set (see Figure 8.2) information should also include the control objectives being addressed and perhaps even the conditions under which the questions are asked.

(c) The user should be able to investigate the relevant question set by asking for amplification on each question and by choosing to reject any particular questions thought to be inappropriate.

(d) The kind of user interface offered by a SUN or Macintosh-type workstation would be preferable to that provided by SAVOIR on a PC.

(e) The phase breakdown of the change control area was appropriate.

(f) The role of 'contexts' was uncertain. However, there seemed to be some link between these and report headings.

(g) There seem to be mappings between the following classes: questions − control objectives − control standards − contexts.

(h) The knowledge elicitation process seems to work by identifying control objectives through first accessing questions.

(i) In asking his question the expert short-cuts or bypasses explicit consideration of the control objective.

(j) The idea that the applicability of questions was a function of the company profile and interviewee class was appropriate.

(k) Two kinds of 'goal' seem to come out of the process of focusing upon the auditor's questions: control objectives and business risks.

(l) The client or user may obtain two kinds of advice associated with these two types of goal.

The 'implementation' phase was then addressed. The accumulated set of questions associated with implementation were considered in terms of the conditions under which they should be asked and also the consequences to the high-level goal 'implementation controls risk' should the answers be unfavourable. A network between this high-level goal and the questions was established although consideration of the relative magnitudes of the various weightings involved was deferred to the next meeting.

INTERVIEW No. 1.13
The object of this interview was to investigate the nature of the conclusions about the implementation phase of change control as a

function of the five principal questions identified as being relevant to this phase.

The discussion centred around the conditions under which each of the five main and seven supplementary questions would be asked. It was found that the reviewer's motivation for asking a question was driven partly by direct control evaluation issues and partly by a more diffuse desire for confirmatory fact-gathering.

Having established a network representing which questions were asked and under what conditions, attention was directed to establishing the relative importance of the five principal questions. To this end the expert was asked, 'how important (on a scale of 1 to 10) is question Q_i?'. This approach, however, was not fruitful, apparently because too many variables were being addressed at the same time, and a consistent set of numbers was not established. As a second approach the expert was asked, 'how worried would you be (on a scale of 1 to 10) if the answer to Q_i was "no" and the answer to the remaining four questions was "yes"?'. The idea behind this approach was to address the separate questions as if they and their influence on the final evaluation were mutually independent. This attempt was more fruitful and was extended by the expert being asked, 'how worried would you be (on a scale of 1 to 10) if the answers to only Q_i and Q_j were "no" and those to the remaining three were all "yes"?'. What emerged out of this line of enquiry was that the answer to this question could be predicted with good accuracy by the following relationship:

$$w(Q_i, Q_j) = \max[w(Q_i), w(Q_j)]$$

where both Q_i and Q_j addressed preventive controls, otherwise

$$w(Q_i, Q_j) = w(Q_i) + w(Q_j)$$

It was speculated that this might suggest the following general hypothesis:

$$w(Q_1, Q_2, \ldots, Q_n) = \max[\{w(Q_{preventive})\}] + \text{SUM}[\{w(Q_{detective})\}]$$

where $w(\{Q_i\})$ is a 'worry' function associated with the answers to the set $\{Q_i\}$ being 'no' (the answers to the complement of the set being 'yes'). A distinction is made between questions which address the quality of preventive controls and those that address the quality of detective controls.

INTERVIEW No. 1.14
The implementation questions were re-addressed, and the expert was asked to explain why the questions would be put.

Two case studies were then inspected. In the first it was found that an evaluation of the implementation controls was always closely linked to other phases. The expert presented the second case study as an apparent exception to the rules so far derived. Upon analysis, this case study clearly revealed the assumptions underlying the existing rules so enabling them to be reclassified.

INTERVIEW No. 1.15
In this session the knowledge engineer and the expert attempted to run a case study through the software model. The expert's immediate responses were first that he needed to ask further questions (i.e. ones not in the system), and second, that much of his evidence was visual, e.g. obtained by looking around the operations room of a client's installation.

First Expert: Epilogue
At this point the firm providing the first expert considered that enough time had been provided to the project and the interviews were drawn to a close.

Before the interviews were wound up the firm agreed to provide confidential access to its official checklist. However, since the knowledge elicitation sessions had virtually ended it was too late to take advantage of this offer. It was clear that access to this material at the beginning of the elicitation process would have allowed much faster progress. An established and already refined body of expertise upon which to focus the discussions would have been a useful starting point. At the very least, it would not have been necessary to spend time generating the relatively high-level questions that were created. Subsequently the expert observed that he often found himself avoiding telling the knowledge engineer things that he (the expert) knew were in his firm's confidential checklist, which was, with hindsight, an understandable reaction. This observation suggests that the interviews would have been more productive had the expert felt less constrained. More importantly, it emphasises the importance of working in an environment where there are no barriers caused by confidentiality issues. Despite this, the interviews with the first expert were a very rich learning experience, for reasons discussed in Section 8.4.

8.3 The Second Expert

The second firm was more circumspect about committing time to the project and agreed to a fixed number of ten interviews, later increased to thirteen.

In an effort to constrain the domain it was decided that the interviews should be limited to clients with IBM System 34 installations. The main reason for this choice was that this particular configuration was practically obsolete among the clients of accounting firms and so any information released about it through the research project was not likely to deprive the participating firm of any competitive advantage.

Given the choice of domain the firm had no qualms about letting the knowledge engineer use its in-house checklist on a confidential basis.

The interviews (second expert)

INTERVIEW No. 2.1
The firm's checklist was used as a focus and the initial discussion centred on how it was used, by whom and also upon its general structure.

The possibility was raised of the author being taken on an IBM System 34 review in order to witness at first hand the environment in which the expertise being addressed by the proposed system was exhibited.

The expert was invited to talk in general terms about a typical IBM System 34 review. He covered such topics as: the reason for the review, preparation for the review, initial fact-gathering, forming an overview, addressing general concerns, the nature of the client personnel to be interviewed, and the possible outcomes of the review.

It was decided that the sub-domain of change control would be addressed.

INTERVIEW No. 2.2
The subset of checklist change control questions was analysed for explanations, associated control objectives and business risks.

A case study was then inspected. The expert gave some background to the client and then went through the checklist questions.

A second case study was inspected.

INTERVIEW No. 2.3
The two case studies were revisited in order to complete unanswered and partially answered questions. A third case study was addressed.

INTERVIEW No. 2.4
It was decided that it was not possible to come to a judgement based upon the limited set of change control questions because the latter had connections with many other areas of the review. It was therefore decided to repeat the first case study but with the intention of performing a complete review, i.e. going through all the sections of the checklist.

INTERVIEW No. 2.5
The case study was continued.

INTERVIEW No. 2.6
The case study was concluded.

INTERVIEW No. 2.7
Questions arising out of the previous meeting were clarified. The overall evaluation for the case study was considered. The business risks associated with the case study were considered. The report deriving from the case study was considered and analysed.

INTERVIEW No. 2.8
It was noted that it had taken four interviews (i.e. about 8–10 hours) to go through a single case study. It was therefore decided to limit the application domain to physical security and logical access controls. This choice was made because it was felt that this area was reasonably self-contained. The nature of the controls in relation to other controls were considered; e.g. controls may be considered as being necessary, sufficient, compensating, or enhancing.

The nature of the advice and conclusions delivered was considered.

A case study was begun. The chosen subset of questions was scrutinised in order to discover if there were any answers which should have defaults by virtue of the installation being an IBM System 34. Software access controls (a subset of physical security and logical access controls) was addressed. The expert felt he needed to cover password administration before giving a judgement.

The expert was not happy about using the general, high-level questions for specific questioning.

The interdependence of the questions was considered and, in particular, which controls compensated for which other controls.

INTERVIEW No. 2.9
The issue of utilities was addressed in the current case study.

INTERVIEW No. 2.10
The general software access control questions were considered for their IBM System 34 defaults and equivalents.

INTERVIEW No. 2.11
The most recent software model was scrutinised, incorporating the work covered so far. The expert was invited to give detailed comments as to his preferences for the user interface characteristics.

INTERVIEW No. 2.12
The knowledge engineer brought a software model to the expert who dismissed it as inappropriate ('I just don't do it that way!'). The knowledge engineer then cleared the computer memory and invited the expert to tell him how he did do it. The expert articulated a model which was input directly into the computer by the knowledge engineer. This process appeared fruitful, which was surprising considering that it went against the common wisdom of how to build an expert system prototype.

INTERVIEW No. 2.13
The above process was continued and concluded.

8.4   Summary of the Process

The first expert

A graphical summary of the events as experienced with the first expert is presented in Figure 8.3.

The interviews are notable for the presence of three kinds of event: repeated domain sub-division, the sudden emergence of control knowledge, and the beginnings of formalised knowledge elicitation.

Domain sub-division

The first expert, who was very cooperative, was always able to articulate at length on any topic presented to him. This meant that in the early stages when the overall application domain (non-processing controls) was being discussed, the 'size' or 'granularity' of the participant concepts was too large for the purposes of the knowledge engineer. Nevertheless, the discussion itself proved valuable by enabling the application domain to be divided into sub-areas. Having narrowed the focus of the elicitation to one of these sub-areas (change control), the above process was repeated giving rise to an appointed sub-sub-area (the implementation phase of change control). The granularity of the participating concepts at this stage was sufficiently small to allow representation within an expert system shell.

An indication of the appropriateness of the scope of the sub-domain seemed to be provided by addressing case studies. At too high a level, case study inspection generated only a series of 'digressions' into general principles. It was only after two domain subdivisions that the treatment of case studies gave rise to appropriately sized 'chunks' of knowledge which could be reasonably expressed in production rules.

The emergence of control knowledge

Early attempts at a graphical representation of the emerging knowledge centred on specific aspects of the review process (see Figure 8.1). However, performing the urgently required review (Interview 2.7) seemed to clear the way for a different type of graph in which the elements represented objects not specific to computer installation reviews. What appears to have crystallised out is a control model of the audit review process. It was found relatively straightforward to implement this model in expert system shell software.

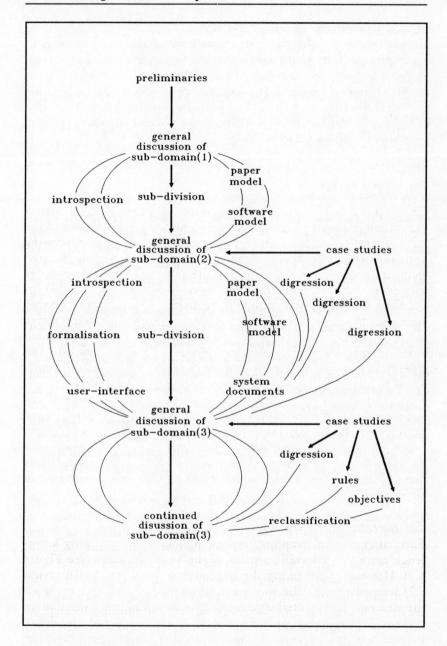

Figure 8.3 Early knowledge elicitation.

The formalisation of knowledge elicitation
Having established the above structure it was a short step to designing a question form that could act as the focus for a semi-automated mode of knowledge elicitation. This method seemed to lend clarity to the elicitation process. The experience of this research led the author (Edwards) to reflect that perhaps a principal role of the knowledge engineer is as a designer of formal, domain specific knowledge elicitation methods.

The second expert

Despite the fact that the domain was consciously narrowed down at the outset (to IBM System 34 installations), the problems of domain scope and boundedness still arose, necessitating what essentially were several restarts of the elicitation process. This experience served to underscore how important an early and thorough feasibility study or application assessment is before any serious elicitation is attempted.

It was interesting to discover that it was not possible to begin with the second expert where the first expert had left off. A period of adjustment to the elicitation process was necessary for both.

In the end, having finally achieved an application domain of manageable scope and definition, the knowledge engineer found that an effective strategy was to represent the expert's statements as he made them using appropriate software (the shell CRYSTAL2 was being used at this point). It had earlier been assumed that this approach would not work. Nevertheless, it did. The lesson here seems to be that one should not assume that any particular technique is universally good or bad but that different approaches work under different conditions.

No user community was established for model evaluation with either participant firm. However, the project did make use of a technical working party involving members of a number of firms who provided useful if limited input. In particular, at one point, a prototype was distributed to the group for evaluation and the resulting comments were generally unfavourable. It transpired that the author had allowed himself to be drawn into using the shell (CRYSTAL2) as a programming language rather than limiting himself to the high-level functionality of the software. This was a direct result of an assumption that he should be driven by the evolving set of user requirements that was being generated by the technical working party. The time spent programming would have been better employed eliciting and structuring the knowledge. The lessons here are:

(a) A shell should not be used outside the bounds of its high-level functionality.

(b) the *initial* concern of the system designer(s) should be in capturing the knowledge rather than in programming the userinterface.

(c) the tasks of knowledge elicitation/structuring and software engineering/coding should be separated, and preferably divided between different people.

8.5 Summary of Conclusions

There follows a checklist of guidelines for expert system development that were discovered or confirmed.

The prototype domain must be very narrow.
It is easy to come to the premature conclusion that the initially chosen sub-domain is too narrow and thereby broaden it. Once into the process of knowledge elicitation it soon becomes clear, as the layers of knowledge are peeled away, that the narrowest of domains can be very deep.

The prototype domain must be well bounded.
The domain should be fairly self-contained and not have too many connections with other domains. Thus, as a rule, it is easier to implement expert systems in highly technical areas than in areas which require input from a large number of sources. An auditing type function poses problems as an application area because it is not likely to be as self-contained as formal checklists suggest.

The user class must be well defined and narrow.
An operational system will be accepted or rejected on the basis of how it performs with a real user. Given the task that the expert system addresses it is conceivable that there could be a large spectrum of potential users. However, it is unlikely that the same level of dialogue would be suitable for all members of the spectrum. Therefore the designers of the system must have an extremely well-defined idea of the general level of expertise of the prospective user of the system. Research is being pursued in the area of multiple-user systems (e.g. user modelling techniques) but unless such research is the intention of the exercise it is important to define the user narrowly.

The knowledge engineer must meet the domain expert more than half way.
Had the knowledge engineer not been familiar with software management and production practices it is likely that the knowledge elicitation process would have proceeded at a much slower rate and possibly might not have proceeded at all. It would therefore seem necessary for a knowledge engineer to have at least a working knowledge of the language of the application domain for knowledge elicitation to proceed. In other words, the knowledge engineer should be able to meet the expert more than half way in the knowledge of the domain compared with a completely lay person for knowledge elicitation to be effective.

Frequent review is crucial.
This is very important during the production and maintenance of conventional software. It is even more crucial in the case of expert systems development in which the process of change and iteration is inherent.

The task should be neither too long nor too short.
From the experience of this research the knowledge engineer concluded that in the performance of the task being addressed the expert should take not take longer than twenty minutes.

A committed user community is essential.
Generally speaking, the user interface is the single most costly item of an expert system. The design of the user interface is driven by the class of people for whom the system is being constructed, the user group. This group therefore constitutes the source of the 'user requirements' for the system and is crucial to the system's development.

Software implementation early on does not add much to a paper model unless the software used is very flexible.
It is widely thought that the construction of expert systems involves a large element of on-line prototyping. In the present case, with the first expert, expressing the paper model in terms of operating software (e.g. a shell) added little to the conceptual model, although it did serve to confirm or disconfirm assumed capabilities of the software. With the second expert the knowledge engineer found that he could code the expert's articulations straight into a computer. However, the software used in this case (CRYSTAL2) was rather more flexible than that used with the first expert (SAVOIR).

A single-page paper representation is most useful.
The representation of the whole model on a single large sheet of paper was far more convenient than a more detailed model represented on several sheets. This was an experience shared with the first expert only. The second expert was quite happy to work within the framework developed with the first expert.

Most of the early prototyping effort should proceed via the paper representation.
As implied above, too early an involvement with serious software implementation sometimes appears to be counter-productive. However, depending on the flexibility of the software being used, it is sometimes possible to aid the elicitation process using an appropriate shell.

Small, capability proving, software exercises may be useful in the early stages.
While discussing the proposed operational characteristics of the proposed expert system it was found useful to use the available software in order to demonstrate that the implementation of these characteristics was feasible.

Model the control knowledge first.
That is, acquire the procedural (control) knowledge first, followed by the declarative (domain) knowledge. In practice a clear-cut division of activities is not possible and the collection of both procedural and declarative knowledge must proceed together. However, in the early stage of knowledge elicitation the focus should be on the control knowledge, this leading to the early construction of an appropriate paper control model upon which declarative knowledge may be later hung.

The use of case studies.
Case studies are useful for revealing hidden assumptions about existing rules provided that the level of granularity being addressed in the application domain is sufficiently fine. There are two uses for case studies: (i) to discover if the level of granularity being addressed is sufficiently fine (for if it is not then the expert tends to be side-tracked into digressions about general principles), and (ii) to aid the reclassification of existing rules as described above.

Interviews should be short but frequent.
A balance should be struck between the length and frequency of the interviews. If the frequency is too low then the sense of project

momentum and continuity is lost. On the other hand, very short interviews do not give the participants enough time to warm to the task.

The use of a shell should be terminated as soon as its functionality has been exhausted.
Shells are functionally high-level software and are therefore functionally constrained. They are generally useful for getting started on a project and can enable the development team to begin getting to grips with the characteristics and structure of the knowledge being accessed. However, as soon as the user group starts making demands, the chances are that in order to satisfy those demands while using the shell the developers would have to treat the shell as a programming language. It is at this point that the shell loses the productivity advantage of its high-level functionality and becomes a hindrance to the person attempting to develop the required user interface. When this happens the system developers should recognise that it is time to adopt a more appropriate software development tool.

Focus initially on the knowledge, not on the user interface.
To take full advantage of whatever shell is being used at the beginning of a project it should always be used within the bounds of its designed high-level function. Therefore the focus at the beginning should not be on user interface issues but on the knowledge elicitation and knowledge representation aided by the shell in as much as it can (but no more).

The expert auditor cannot always express why he is asking a question but he always knows which question to ask.
This is probably an exaggeration to some degree but by taking this as a principal assumption it was found that the conceptualisation of a paper model and the subsequent knowledge elicitation became much less painful. In other words, it was found useful to focus upon 'the question' as the mediating agent of the expert's knowledge. The question that arises here is, 'to what degree does this principle (if true) have analogues in other application domains?'.

Expert system prototype development.
The kind of knowledge elicitation experience described above is a highly iterative process in which the inputs to many of the phases happen almost simultaneously (see Figure 8.4). A review of the nature of the system function or the user or the user interface at any stage will generate input to an updated functional specification. Considera-

tion of the user or the *modus operandi* of the system provides inputs to the user interface specification.

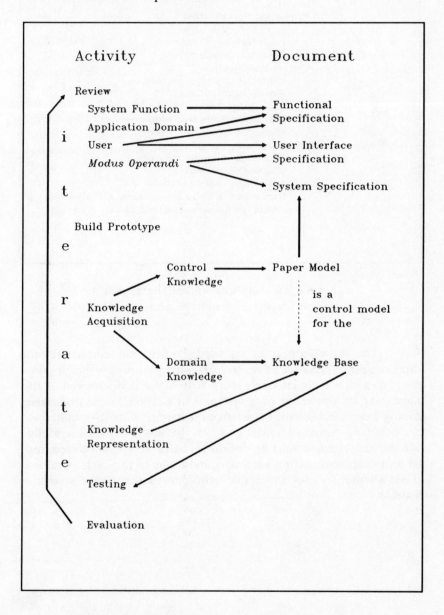

Figure 8.4 Expert system prototype development

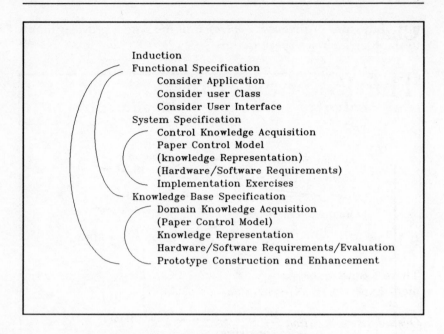

Induction
Functional Specification
     Consider Application
     Consider user Class
     Consider User Interface
System Specification
        Control Knowledge Acquisition
        Paper Control Model
        (knowledge Representation)
        (Hardware/Software Requirements)
        Implementation Exercises
Knowledge Base Specification
        Domain Knowledge Acquisition
        (Paper Control Model)
        Knowledge Representation
        Hardware/Software Requirements/Evaluation
        Prototype Construction and Enhancement

Figure 8.5 Implications for the expert
system life cycle (prototype phase).

The initial aspect of knowledge elicitation emphasises the
capture and expression of control knowledge through the development of a paper model (see Figure 8.5). What is discovered at this
stage may be described in a system specification. A control model
having been established, knowledge elicitation shifts its emphasis to
the details of domain knowledge when the way in which knowledge
is to be represented must be decided. The prototype is refined, tested and evaluated during successive iterations of the cycle until it is
clear whether or not the implementation of the target system is
feasible.

Chapter 9

The Demonstrator

9.1 A Functional Specification

There follows a user view of the Computer Installation Risk Assessment Expert (CIRAX) system and its facilities.

Overall system function
The function of the system is a 'trouble-shooter' in the assessment of business risks associated with computer installations.

The user
The user is envisaged as a senior member of an audit department which would use the system to assess the 'risk level' of aspects of the computer system under scrutiny with a view to establishing a way of directing audit resources to the riskiest areas.

The prototype sub-domain
The essential task being addressed by the system is similar to a computer audit review. The review area is divided into twelve sub-areas:

1. General details
2. Overall management controls
3. System software
4. Physical security and logical access controls
5. Computer operations
6. Data preparation and data control
7. Data files and program libraries
8. Recovery and contingency plans
9. Insurance cover

10. System maintenance and change control procedures
11. System development controls
12. User acceptance testing

Each of these areas is sub-divided into a number of sections. In particular, area 4 (physical security and logical access controls) is sub-divided as follows:

4.2 Environmental controls
4.3 Physical access controls
4.4 Software access controls
4.5 Password administration
4.6 Utilities

(note that the label 4.1 is reserved for dealing with the overall function of area 4).

The prototype sub-domain which CIRAX addresses is that covered by section 4.4, software access controls.

Modus operandi

(a) The user starts the program and is presented with the system header and the three options: 'system information', 'start consultation', and 'exit'. The 'system information' option makes available to the user a facility containing a variety of historical and anecdotal information about the development of the system (see later). The 'exit' option allows the user to quit the program.

(b) Choosing the option 'start consultation' causes the appearance of several form-like screens containing templates for a variety of client details. Particulars such as client name, the year end, the current year, the nature of the business, the manufacturer of the computer being used, and other details about the hardware and software are entered.
  If the user enters 'IBM' for processor manufacturer and 'System 34' for processor model then fields appropriate to this combination are filled with predetermined values in subsequent screens. Otherwise the corresponding fields are left blank. Also, if 'IBM System 34' is chosen, the questions later asked will be very specific to that configuration, otherwise they will be general and address installation-independent control objectives.

(c) The user is then presented with a menu displaying a list of twelve review areas:

1. General details
2. Overall management controls
3. System software
4. Physical security and logical access controls
5. Computer operations
6. Data preparation and data control
7. Data files and program libraries
8. Recovery and contingency plans
9. Insurance cover
10. System maintenance and change control procedures
11. System development controls
12. User acceptance testing

There is an on-line explanation facility for the meaning of the menu entries presented. An 'exit' option is also available, which allows the user to return to the previous menu level. The user will generally choose a review area for investigation. In the present case only area 4 contains any knowledge.

(d) Upon selecting area 4 the user is then informed that the area is sub-divided into the following five sections:

4.2 Environmental controls
4.3 Physical access controls
4.4 Software access controls
4.5 Password administration
4.6 Utilities

Context-dependent explanation facilities are available for each entry in this menu. The user is invited to choose which section or combination of sections to investigate. The only section currently implemented is 4.4, software access controls.

(e) Upon selecting section 4.4 the user is asked an appropriate set of questions that address the issue of software access controls. Explanation, glossary and utilities facilities are available as the questions are being asked and may be invoked at any time (see system facilities and system specification (Appendix E) for details of these).

(f) Once the questions have been asked the 'area' menu returns, at which point the user may, in principle, choose another area for investigation.

(g) Having investigated as many areas (and sections) as required the user then chooses the 'exit' option which causes the display of the menu:

<u>C I R A X</u>
1. Data entry
2. Utilities
3. Quit

The 'data entry' option is, in fact, the one which has just been executed. Choosing the 'utilities' option brings up the following menu:

<u>CIRAX - Utilities Facility</u>
1. Reports and assessments
2. What-if
3. Quit utilities facility
4. Suspend consultation
5. System information

(h) Should the user choose to generate a report (option 'reports and assessments' above) he has two options: an overview or a detailed assessment. The overview report gives a short assessment of the quality of the controls under investigation. The detailed assessment option generates a report that includes commentary about best practice on those areas in which the client's installation has been found wanting. Specific advice is also provided to the user for the benefit of the client. For either report the user is informed about which ascii file to which the report has been written (details of report generation may be found the system specification)

(i) Having generated a report, the user might wish to see what effect changing the answers to some questions will have. If so he will select the 'what-if' option. Upon doing so the user is again prompted to choose an area and a combination of sections; the answered questions are listed on the screen together with their current answers (or 'values'). The user is invited to change whichever answers (if any) he sees fit. As before, the user may continue, in principle, with the 'what-if' facility but with respect to other areas and sections.

(j) Once the user has changed all the answers that he wants he must 'exit' from the what-if area selection menu and he is warned that he may be required to answer additional questions as a result of some original responses being changed.

(k) At this point the user may choose to enter 'utilities' and generate another report or suspend the consultation.

System facilities

System information
The system information facility provides the user with a menu-driven series of screens containing information about the history of the project as well as commentary on some of the problems encountered. A brief account of the structure of the system is provided, as well as an indication of the effect that use of the particular software had on that structure.

Glossary
The glossary is a menu-driven series of nested screens giving explanations and definitions of the various terms which are used in conjunction with various hardware–software configurations (in this case the IBM System 34). The glossary is available whenever a question is being asked.

Explanation
Associated with each question is an explanation that may use some of the terms available in the glossary.

9.2 A Sample Consultation and Report

Reproduced below is an example of a consultation conducted with CIRAX, followed by the management report generated by the system.

A sample CIRAX consultation

```
            Welcome to CIRAX
            ----------------

        - a  C  omputer
             I  nstallation
             R  isk
             A  ssessment
          e  X  pert

  system information   start consultation   exit
```

The user decides to initiate a consultation with the system.

```
  Client Details
  --------------


  Name:   Bloggs and Co.
  Y/E:    September 14th
  Year:   1988

  Nature of Business:
  The manufacture and distribution of
  high quality widgets.
```

The system retrieves information pertinent to the client (who, in this case, already exists on file)

```
  Machine - Hardware (1)

  Processor:

  Manufacturer:    IBM
  Model:           System 34
  No. Units:
  Size:

                        Explain (Y/N) ?  N
```

Any changes to the client's computer system configuration may be recorded here. Explanation about terms is also available.

```
  Machine - Hardware (2)

  Disk Units:

  Manufacturer:    IBM
  Model:           (a hard fixed disk)
  No. Units:       1
  Size:            256 mbytes
```

```
Machine - Hardware (3)

Tape Units:

Manufacturer:
Model:
No. Units:
Size:            ████████████████████████
```

```
Machine - Hardware (4)

Printers:

Manufacturer:   IBM
Model:          7520
No. Units:      1███████████████████████
```

```
Machine - Hardware (5)

Terminals:

Manufacturer:   IBM
Model:          5022
No. Units:      6███████████████████████████
```

```
Machine - System Software (1)

O/S: SSP              Version:

Other System Software:

Data File Utility        Sort Utility
Source Entry Utility     Work Station Utility
Patch Procedure
                         Explain (Y/N)? N
```

```
    Please select the area that you wish to
    investigate:

    1. General Details (mandatory 1st time in)          The user decides to use
    2. Overall Management Controls                      the explanation facility.
    3. System Software
    4. Phys. Security & Logical Access Controls
    5. Computer Operations
    6. Data Preparation and Data Control
       (next screen ...)                    explain
```

```
    Please select the area that you wish explained.

    1. General Details (mandatory 1st time in)
    2. Overall Management Controls
    3. System Software
    4. Phys. Security & Logical Access Controls
    5. Computer Operations
    6. Data Preparation and Data Control


                                             exit
```

```
    4. Physical Security and Logical Access Controls
    ----------------------------------------------

    This area checks to see if there are sufficient       The explanation available
    physical and logical access controls, together        for 'Physical Security and
    with appropriate environmental controls, to reduce    Logical Access Controls'
    to an acceptable level the risk of unauthorised       is displayed.
    access to information and of damage to or
    disruption of computer facilities.
```

```
    Please select the area that you wish explained.

    1. General Details (mandatory 1st time in)
    2. Overall Management Controls                        Leaving the local
    3. System Software                                    explanation facility.
    4. Phys. Security & Logical Access Controls
    5. Computer Operations
    6. Data Preparation and Data Control


       (next screen ...)                    exit
```

```
    Please select the area that you wish to
    investigate:

 1. General Details (mandatory 1st time in)
 2. Overall Management Controls
 3. System Software
 4. Phys. Security & Logical Access Controls
 5. Computer Operations
 6. Data Preparation and Data Control
       (next screen ...)                explain
```

The user chooses to
investigate section 4.

```
PHYSICAL SECURITY AND LOGICAL ACCESS CONTROLS
is sub-divided into the following subobjectives.
Please choose one (* indicates Selected):
                                        Explain
        4.2  ENVIRONMENTAL CONTROLS
        4.3  PHYSICAL ACCESS CONTROLS
        4.4  SOFTWARE ACCESS CONTROLS
        4.5  PASSWORD ADMINISTRATION
        4.6  UTILITIES
                                        Proceed
```

An explanation about
'Software Access Controls'
is requested ...

```
    4.4 SOFTWARE ACCESS CONTROLS
    ------------------------

    There should be adequate software access
    controls to protect the production data files
    and applications software against unauthorised
    access, misuse and/or manipulation.
```

... and obtained.

```
PHYSICAL SECURITY AND LOGICAL ACCESS CONTROLS
is sub-divided into the following subobjectives.
Please choose one (* indicates Selected):
                                        Explain
        4.2  ENVIRONMENTAL CONTROLS
        4.3  PHYSICAL ACCESS CONTROLS
        4.4  SOFTWARE ACCESS CONTROLS
        4.5  PASSWORD ADMINISTRATION
        4.6  UTILITIES
                                        Proceed
```

Section 4.4 is nominated
for investigation.

```
PHYSICAL SECURITY AND LOGICAL ACCESS CONTROLS
is sub-divided into the following subobjectives.
Please choose one (* indicates Selected):
                                        Explain
        4.2  ENVIRONMENTAL CONTROLS
        4.3  PHYSICAL ACCESS CONTROLS
*       4.4  SOFTWARE ACCESS CONTROLS
        4.5  PASSWORD ADMINISTRATION
        4.6  UTILITIES
                                        Proceed
```

The system is advised
to proceed.

```
                              (4.4.za1a)

    Is sign-on security used for all users?




    Yes    No    Unknown        Explain   Glossary
                                          Utilities
```

The user is asked the
first question but decides
he wants some explanation.

```
Sign-On Security (screen 1)
----------------
Each user on an IBM System/34 computer has a user
profile that consists of a user identification,
his password, details of his badge (if any),
special authorities (needed to perform operating
functions), an initial program to be called when
he signs on, and details of files and programs
authorised for use.
                            More?   Yes   No
```

The concept of 'sign-on'
is explained to the user.

```
Sign-On Security (screen 2)
----------------
A person who starts to use the IBM System 34 will
be prompted for an identification and then for his
badge (if badges are in use) and finally for a
password. Thus at its simplest the password/badge
security provide the overall access controls.
They are important because they allow the unique
identification of a user and therefore the
definition of access rights that are ...   (cont)
```

```
Sign-On Security (screen 3)
----------------
... appropriate to that particular user
(determined by the client according to a user's
responsibilities within the organisation) - in IBM
terminology a security profile . This simple
procedure to log on to the computer provides the
basis of controls that are vital from the audit
standpoint.
                              More?   Yes   No
```

```
Sign-On Security (screen 4)
----------------
If a company does not have good control procedures
designed to ensure the continuing confidentiality
of passwords, and controls to ensure that profiles
remain appropriate to users current functions the
effectiveness of much of the other software access
control procedures will be undermined.
```

```
                              (4.4.za1a)

     Is sign-on security used for all users?



     Yes    No    Unknown       Explain  Glossary
                                         Utilities
```

The first question is
re-asked and this time
is answered.

```
                              (4.4.za2a)

     Is menu security used?



     Yes    No    Unknown       Explain  Glossary
                                         Utilities
```

The next question.

(4.4.za2b)

Are all users, including computer operators,
restricted to only those facilities they
require for the performance of their duties
by the use of mandatory menus?

And the next - but
explanation is requested.

Yes   No   Unknown   Explain Glossary
                                        Utilities

(4.4.za2b)

Just because menu security is used there is
no guarantee that it enforces segregation
of function. Therefore this question must
be asked.

Explanation terminated.

More?   Yes   No

(4.4.za2b)

Are all users, including computer operators,
restricted to only those facilities they
require for the performance of their duties
by the use of mandatory menus?

Yes   No   Unknown   Explain Glossary
                                        Utilities

(4.4.za3a)

Is the resource security used to protect
access to sensitive program libraries
and data files?

An alternative means of
accessing information is
via the glossary.

Yes   No   Unknown   Explain Glossary
                                        Utilities

```
Sign-On  Security      System       Operator
Menu     Security      Display Station Operator
Resource Security      SECPROF
Owner    Access        SECRES
Change   Access        SEU
Read     Access
Execute  Access
Master Security Officer
Security        Officer
                                        Exit
```

'Resource Security' is chosen from the glossary.

```
RESOURCE SECURITY (screen 1) - Files and Libraries

Resource security is designed to protect files,
libraries, and peripherals. A file might be a
collection of data relating to sales ledger
masterfile information. A library is typically a
file, containing program source code, job control
procedures, executable program code, program
subroutines or module program source code, job
control procedures, and directories ...   (cont)
```

```
RESOURCE SECURITY (screen 2) - Files and Libraries

... of these components.

The resource security is defined in terms of
access rights, either by user ID's (specific
access) and/or the access of all users (called
public access). The rights granted can also be
divided into a number of types of access: ...
                                        (cont)
```

```
RESOURCE SECURITY (screen 3) - Files and Libraries

... Owner , Change , Read , and Execute .

Resource security is mediated via the  SECRES
file.




                        More?   Yes   No
```

RESOURCE SECURITY (screen 4) Devices as Resources

Resource security allows each device to be
controlled in the same manner as a library or
file. In this way it is possible for a user to be
excluded from particular terminals. For example
this can be of particular use where one wishes to
restrict the operation of the payroll to a
terminal designated for payroll purposes.

More?   Yes   No

RESOURCE SECURITY (screen 5) - Its application

The fact that all programs and data files are
essentially files (possibly controlled within
libraries) means that resource security can be
used to provide a sophisticated method of access
controls. However the control afforded is heavily
dependent upon the care exercised when setting up
the manner in which files/libraries are stored.

More?   Yes   No

RESOURCE SECURITY (screen 6) - Its application

Resource security will typically be used to
provide separate areas for each of the main
accounting functions (e.g. payroll, nominal
ledger, sales ledger, purchase ledger) and these
will be structured to ensure that live software
and data are separate. In addition to the main
accounting areas separate areas will also be
established so that utilities, ...   (cont)

RESOURCE SECURITY (screen 7) - Its application

programming tools (such as the editor, SEU , and
the compiler, typically RPG) and programs
currently being maintained are kept in separate
development areas. The aim being to provide
resource security, based around the protection of
groups of resources that reflect different
operations of the company (sales/purchases) or
different types of ...   (cont)

RESOURCE SECURITY (screen 8) - Its application

... entity on the computer (data/programs).

In practice most clients do not take full
advantage of the resource security facilities and
it is common to see just a few libraries which all
members of staff have access. The clients tend to
rely on menu security and make little use of
resource security.

```
Sign-On  Security      System            Operator
Menu     Security      Display Station Operator
Resource Security      SECPROF
Owner    Access        SECRES
Change   Access        SEU
Read     Access
Execute  Access
Master Security Officer
Security        Officer
                                    Exit
```

                                        (4.4.za3a)

Is the resource security used to protect
access to sensitive program libraries   Back to the consultation.
and data files?

Yes   No   Unknown   Explain Glossary
                                      Utilities

                                        (4.4.za3b)

Considering that resource security is not
used are there any compensating procedures,
(apart from the use of application specific
passwords) to protect sensitive program files
and libraries?

Yes   No   Unknown   Explain Glossary
                                      Utilities

```
                                    (4.4.za4)

        Is access to sensitive functions or
        resources further restricted by the use of
        application specific passwords?



        Yes    No    Unknown      Explain   Glossary
                                           Utilities
```

```
        Please select the area that you wish to
        investigate:

     1. General Details (mandatory 1st time in)        Questioning has ended.
     2. Overall Management Controls
     3. System Software
     4. Phys. Security & Logical Access Controls
     5. Computer Operations
     6. Data Preparation and Data Control
        (next screen ...)                    explain
```

```
        (... continued)

     7.  Data Files and Program Libraries
     8.  Recovery and Contingency Plans
     9.  Insurance Cover
     10. System Maintenance and Change Control
     11. System Development Controls
     12. User Acceptance Testing

        Exit        (previous screen)        explain
```

```
                C I R A X
                ---------

                1. Data Entry                The user selects
                2. Utilities                 'Utilities' ...
                3. Quit
```

```
CIRAX - Utilities Facility
--------------------------

1. Reports and Assessments
2. What-If
3. Quit Utilities Facility
4. Suspend Consultation
5. System Information
```

... and then asks for
'Reports and Assessments'
...

```
CIRAX - Reports and Assessments
-------------------------------

1. Quick Overview
2. Detailed Assessment
3. Exit
```

... and in particular for
a 'Detailed Assessment'...

```
You may find your report on the file

        detailed.prn
```

... at which point a
report is generated.

```
CIRAX - Reports and Assessments
-------------------------------

1. Quick Overview
2. Detailed Assessment
3. Exit
```

```
CIRAX - Utilities Facility
--------------------------

1. Reports and Assessments
2. What-If
3. Quit Utilities Facility
4. Suspend Consultation
5. System Information
```

```
   C I R A X
   ---------

1. Data Entry
2. Utilities
3. Quit
```

```
Thank you for using CIRAX.
```

The detailed report generated by this consultation session appears on the following pages.

The Detailed Report

CONTROLS RISK AND BUSINESS RISK ASSESSMENT REPORT

As a result of our review of the System 34 installation at the site of the client Bloggs and Co. for the year 1988 ending on September 14th we have the following comments on software access controls.

OVERALL ASSESSMENT
The software access controls have been found to be barely adequate since:
• sign on security is used
• menu security is used
• resource security is not used
• resource security is not covered

DETAILED ASSESSMENT

To ensure the continued smooth running of computer operations and the production of accurate information it is essential that the integrity of both programs and data files is maintained. This requires adequate controls to ensure the prevention of unauthorised updates to either live data or programs.

We believe that there are some deficiencies in the relevant procedures which are currently in force. Each of these is discussed in the ensuing paragraphs.

The System 34 provides two types of security; sign-on security and file/library (resource) security. The former governs user access to the system and may include restrictions to particular program menus (menu security). The latter can be used to restrict access to designated files and program libraries. In addition, individual applications may have their own passwords associated with them.

The use of sign-on security is absolutely essential in any installation. The absence of this fundamental control virtually precludes attempts to introduce other compensatory controls.

Sign-on security permits the use of mandatory menus (menu security) so that users may be constrained in which system software they can access by virtue of their security profile which is determined by the attributes assigned to their user identification by the appropriate authority in their organisation.

In addition to access control via mandatory menus a user may also be constrained access by controls placed on the software itself. Thus a particular package may be accessible by particular users, this access being determined at the software rather than at the user.

Finally, individual programs may have passwords associated with them designed to control those who might wish to execute them.

Resource Security

Using file and library security (resource security) it is possible to protect particular files and/or program libraries by restricting access to them to designated users only. Four categories of authority may be given to a user:

(i) Execute: user may run programs from the protected library.
(ii) Read: user has execute authority and may also display the contents of the file or library.
(iii) Change: user has read authority and may also create, delete or amend the contents of the protected file or library.
(iv) Owner: user has change level access and may also grant access to other users or rename the file/library.

The client has indicated that resource security is not used to protect access to sensitive program libraries and data files and in so doing may be incurring risk even though menu security is being used.

BUSINESS RISKS

The business risks so far addressed are associated with the quality of the software access controls. Since the level of software access control has been found to be only moderate there is some degree of risk to be associated with *error, fraud* and the *unauthorised disclosure of information*. These are in the main due to: a lack of attention to resource security.

Chapter 10

The Tools Used

10.1 Introduction

The two expert system shell products used during the course of this work were SAVOIR and CRYSTAL. This section provides the flavour of a comparison between the two. It should be noted that the comments made are illustrative and in no way exhaustive.

SAVOIR and CRYSTAL differ in their user interface characteristics and in the detail of their inference mechanisms but they both use production rules as their method of representing knowledge. This means that it is possible to treat both products as members of the same class and therefore draw comparisons between them.

The operation of a production system may be considered in terms of the high-level assertions in which a user might be interested. These high-level assertions, or goals, represent the space of possible solutions to a problem (strictly speaking, this is true only for problem types with a limited solution space). The objective of the inference is to discover the logical values of the goals. Generally speaking each goal will depend for its value on the value of other lower level linking assertions, or sub-goals. These sub-goals may be further linked to yet other sub-goals. Goals are related to their sub-goals by production rules. Ultimately the value of the lowest level sub-goals must be obtained by asking the user some questions. The structure beneath a goal therefore resembles a tree in which branch nodes represent assertions and leaves correspond to data supplied by the user.

Both the tools used enable the user to express production rules in an easy way. Once a set of rules has been established the shell uses its own inference engine to make appropriate inferences and also to ask the user for information where necessary.

The following is a simple illustration of an inference net.

```
              A1
            /    \
          B1  and   B2
         /  \         \
       C1  or  c2      n>6
      /
    (d1 and d2) or d3
```

In this example assertions which obtain values through the operation of a rule are denoted by upper-case letters (A1, B1, B2, C1) and those that obtain values through asking the user are lower-case (c2, d1, d2, d3). The production rules represented in the example are as follows:

> A1 is true if B1 is true and B2 is true
> B1 is true if C1 is true or c2 is true
> B2 is true if n is greater than 6
> C1 is true if either both of d1 and d2 are true or if d3 is
>   true

and values for c2, d1, d2 and d3 are obtained by asking the user a question such as, 'is c2 true?'

The objective of this small system is to determine whether A1 is true or false.

A knowledge base may have any number of high-level goals which may be related to one another and to the network of sub-goals and user supplied facts in a very complex manner.

It will now be now explained how the above example is implemented in both SAVOIR and CRYSTAL. It is first necessary, however, to specify the user requirement that after the consultation the user should be informed as to whether A1 is true or false.

10.2 SAVOIR

SAVOIR operates on a compile–execute cycle. That is, the system designer must create a file containing statements in a purpose-designed, high-level language and compile this file using SAVOIR software. The result is an executable module. The SAVOIR code corresponding to the example above is presented below. The clarity of the language is such that the reader can immediately recognise the function of the key words, which appear in capitals, such as INVESTIGATE, ASSOONAS, QUESTION and NUMBER. Execution of the model produced from this code generates a consultation in which the user is asked the minimum number of questions and in an appropriate order enabling a value for A1 to be obtained efficiently.

```
INVESTIGATE A1
ASSOONAS    AT_START

DISPLAY     'A1 has been found to be true'
ASSOONAS    A1

DISPLAY     'A1 has been found to be false'
ASSOONAS    NOT A1

CONDITION   A1 'A1 is true'
            B1 AND B2

CONDITION   B1 'B1 is true'
            C1 OR c2

CONDITION   C1 'C1 is true'
            d1 AND d2 OR d3

CONDITION   B2 'B2 is true'
            n > 6

QUESTION    n
            'What is the value of n?'
            NUMERIC 0 1000

QUESTION    c2
            'Is c2 true?'
            YESNO ONLY

QUESTION    d1
            'Is d1 true?'
            YESNO ONLY

QUESTION    d2
            'Is d2 true?'
            YESNO ONLY

QUESTION    d3
            'Is d3 true?'
            YESNO ONLY
```

10.3 CRYSTAL2

CRYSTAL differs from SAVOIR in that it is totally interactive. There is no compile–execute cycle and the user may change something and run the result without delay. The system designer is not responsible for the maintenance of a source file containing the knowledge base. This function is catered for by the CRYSTAL software itself. This has the time-saving advantage indicated but suffers from the disadvantage that the user has little control over the form of the documented version of the knowledge base.

Upon starting CRYSTAL the user is presented with a screen with the legend 'CRYSTAL MASTER RULE' which corresponds to the top of an inference tree as described above. Every CRYSTAL screen is labelled with the assertion currently being developed. The user may express this assertion as a disjunction of conjunctions. For example, in

> U
> > if X1 and X2 and X3
> > or Y1 and Y2 and Y3
> > or Z1 and Z2 and Z3

the assertion U is a disjunction of the conjunctions (X1 and X2 and X3), (Y1 and Y2 and Y3), and (Z1 and Z2 and Z3).
Every assertion in CRYSTAL is expressed in this way.

In the present case the following rule was effectively implemented:

> CRYSTAL MASTER RULE
> if A1 and   Display: A1 has been found to be true
> > or   Display: A1 has been found to be false

Here, if A1 turns out to be true then a message is put out to that effect; otherwise the message 'A1 has been found to be false' is displayed. (It should be pointed out that the above is not CRYSTAL code.) This is one of the ways in which the user can introduce procedural code into a model, that is, make the computer execute actions in sequence.

Having completed the structure of the current assertion (in this case the CRYSTAL MASTER RULE) the user then selects one of the newly participant assertions and develops that in the same way. In this manner a the tree structure described above may be completed.

Upon running the program the user is asked for the values of the lower-level assertions that the system requires in order to infer the value of the higher-level goals. Eventually the top-level goal takes on a value.

The generated CRYSTAL code corresponding to the above example is reproduced below.

```
[  1]  A1 is true
        + IF    [  2] B1 is true
        +  AND [  3] B2 is true

[  2]  B1 is true
        + IF    [  4] C1 is true
        + OR    [  5] c2 is true

[  3]  B2 is true
          IF    DO: Display Form
                    What is the value of n?
                        <n>
          AND   DO: Test Expression
                    n > 6
[  4]  C1 is true
        + IF    [  6] d1 is true
        +  AND [  7] d2 is true
        + OR    [  8] d3 is true

[  5]  c2 is true
          IF    DO: Yes/No Question
                    Is c2 true?

[  6]  d1 is true
          IF    DO: Yes/No Question
                    Is d1 true?

[  7]  d2 is true
          IF    DO: Yes/No Question
                    Is d2 true?

[  8]  d3 is true
          IF    DO: Yes/No Question
                    Is d3 true?

[  9]              CRYSTAL  MASTER  RULE
        + IF    [  1] A1 is true
          AND   DO: Display Form
                    A1 has been found to be true.
          OR    DO: Display Form
                    A1 has been found to be false.
```

This code is fairly readable. However CRYSTAL always arranges the items in alphabetical order so that should a user require a more logical ordering he has to think carefully about the names given to

the various assertions. This becomes very tedious. CRYSTAL is
therefore effectively a totally interactive tool.

10.4 Which Shell was Best?

The huge advantage that CRYSTAL2 has over SAVOIR is that it is
extremely easy to learn for two reasons. First, it is interactive and its
user-interface is extremely well designed. During the construction of
a model the user always knows from the information on the screen
what is expected of him. Second, it is based on a very simple model,
i.e. that of a simple decision tree.

To construct a SAVOIR model the user must effectively learn
a computer language and then write a program in it. Consequently
the learning curve for SAVOIR is much shallower than that for
CRYSTAL2. However, the system designer has much more control
over the structure of the documented form of a SAVOIR knowledge
base. It is easy to imagine how unwieldy a large CRYSTAL2 model
could become. With SAVOIR the designer has the option of structuring the knowledge base so that the corresponding hard copy is
readable and therefore more easily maintainable.

SAVOIR supports a variety of important facilities that CRYS-
TAL2 does not, such as forward (as well as backward) chaining, the
values 'known' and 'answered' for assertions, the ability to go back
to the previous question, nested explanation trails, and an inbuilt
help facility. These and many other characteristics make SAVOIR the
more powerful tool even though it is harder to come to grips with
at the onset.

Chapter 11

Conclusion

11.1 The Constraints Revisited

We are now in a position to reconsider, with hindsight, decisions taken at the outset of the project.

(a) *The application domain*
It had been decided that this would be 'the assessment of business risks associated with computer installations'. It turned out that this domain was of huge scope and that in attempting to narrow it down to a sub-domain that could be reasonably addressed as a prototype the resulting sub-area was too small to be of much use. It also became evident that the domain was richly interconnected, that is, it was not well bounded. 'Well boundedness' is generally agreed to be a prerequisite for an appropriate application domain for expert system development.

(b) *The use of PC-based shells*
As discussed elsewhere in this book, using an expert system shell during the early part of model development is an efficient and effective way of achieving familiarity with the structure of the problem being addressed. However, as soon as the user community begins to refine its demands on the user interface, a shell is increasingly unlikely to be able to support the functionality required unless it is used more as a programming language than as a high-level tool. It is at this point that a shell loses the productivity advantage associated with its expressive power and a system designer should consider writing a purpose-built shell for the class of problem under investigation.

(c) *Multiple experts*

Although it was initially thought feasible for several experts to be included in the knowledge elicitation process it was ultimately found possible to involve only two experts in the time available, and even this number served to overstretch resources from the point of view of maximising research output.

It took approximately the same amount of time to establish a rapport and a working routine with each of the experts; it was not possible to start with the second expert at the point at which one had left off with the first. Also, it did not seem feasible, given the sensitivity exhibited by both participant firms, to arrange for a true, round-table, multi-expert approach.

The knowledge engineer's experience with both experts was that after about ten meetings (by which time the problems associated with the scope and boundedness of the domain had been dealt with) the knowledge elicitation process suddenly became much more productive. In terms of producing a demonstrator the project would have progressed further had only one expert been used. However, the use of two experts proved useful in terms of other aspects of the research. In particular, the time spent with the first expert in developing the control model and the initial prototype was well worthwhile.

11.2 A Summary of Development Guidelines

From the experience gained in this project it is appropriate to summarise the main findings as a list of recommendations to those Institute members who are thinking of building expert systems.

(a) The prototype sub-domain must be extremely narrow.
(b) The prototype sub-domain must be well bounded.
(c) An applications assessment exercise designed to ensure that (a) and (b) are true should be initiated before a decision is made to proceed with prototype development.
(d) The user class for the system must be well defined and narrow.
(e) The knowledge engineer should have, at the outset, a working familiarity with the language of the expert in the application domain.

(f) The use of a single-page paper representation is an effective modelling aid.

(g) If high-level software (e.g. an expert system shell) is used, its use should cease as soon as its functionality has been exhausted and the question of what is a more appropriate tool or language should be addressed.

(h) Frequent review of the knowledge engineering process provides insight into the suitability of the methods adopted.

(i) Case studies are useful for revealing hidden assumptions in the expert's reasoning provided that the conceptual level being addressed is sufficiently low.

(j) Conversely, the application of case studies can be used as a test to discover if the conceptual level being addressed is sufficiently low. If it is not then the expert has a tendency to digress into discussions of general principles.

(k) The expert must be cooperative in articulating his knowledge and be unconstrained either on his own part or on the part of his organisation.

(l) The expert's superiors must be fully committed to the exercise.

(m) The task chosen should take no more than half an hour for an expert to perform.

(n) Frequent but generally brief contact between knowledge engineer and expert is probably better than infrequent but long interviews.

(o) A committed user community for providing feedback on the developing system is crucial.

(p) Caution should be exercised before adopting a multi-expert approach. If it is, then one expert should be considered as 'knowledge-czar' and be responsible for taking final decisions about the contents of the knowledge base.

11.3 Conclusion – A Concept Proven?

It is worthwhile at this stage to recapitulate the characteristics shared by both experts that were interviewed bearing in mind that these commonalities probably arose, in the main, out of the general auditing culture from which both individuals sprang.

Both experts were deeply involved with question design. The questions ideally would be computer configuration specific but would also be capable of addressing the high-level generic control objectives which form the foci of a computer audit review. Both experts (and their firms) invest a great deal of resources in developing generic checklists which address required computer audit review objectives. However, both firms involved do not seem to be taking the approach of designing computer configuration-specific checklists for addressing these higher-level generic control objectives. This, in effect, is what the prototype expert system developed during the research described here does. The system developed represents an architecture that may be used as a *skills archiving facility*. The particular skills involved here are the identification of those questions which are most appropriate for addressing computer audit review control objectives given the involvement of a specific computer configuration running specific software, and the evaluation of the answers to those questions. A computer audit department will generally contain individuals who are expert with respect to specific computer installations. The particular expertise of these individuals could be archived on such a system as the one developed. An accumulating knowledge base of such expertise would be a valuable resource at least for the staff of the general audit department who often have to consult the computer audit department on such matters.

Appendix A

A Survey of Decision Support Systems in Accounting

A.1 Introduction

This survey examines the current state of decision support systems in accounting and finance functions. The orientation differs from studies in this field carried out previously (Grinyer 1983, MacGregor 1982, for example). As part of a larger project looking at expert systems in accounting, it was hoped that a study of the present role of decision support systems would provide an glimpse into the future for expert systems.

For the purposes of this study a decision support system (DSS) is defined as 'any computerised system which provides support for planning or which directly assists management decision making'. Participants in the survey were asked explicitly to exclude from their answers matters relating to low-level transaction processing and clerical tasks. It was felt that information about such systems would not serve as a guide to the potential of expert systems.

Certain authors (Stoner 1984, for example) have characterised DSS and expert systems (ES) as lying on a continuum of degrees of complexity. At one extreme, simple decision support systems are mathematical models with largely numeric outputs, such as a spreadsheet. At the other, complex expert systems may provide diagnosis, advice and even initiate actions using expert knowledge and heuristics. For our purposes, decision support systems were towards the latter end of this range. Any system not concerned with routine transactions processing or exhibiting expert characteristics was considered a DSS.

This appendix was written by John Holt and Philip Powell

This study is based on questionnaires sent to a large group of potential DSS users. The users were divided into three categories: financial/accounting personnel in large industrial firms, smaller accounting practices, and constituents of the twenty largest professional accounting firms. The first group consisted of a stratified sample of 100 firms from the largest 300 of *The Times* 1000 companies, 100 firms from the 700–1000 ranked *The Times* companies, and 100 from the *Kompass* 1000–2000 ranked companies. In all cases the rankings are by turnover for the period in question. These 300 companies received a postal questionnaire.

A postal questionnaire was also sent to 300 accounting practices drawn at random. These practices ranged from one-man operations to large (yet non-top twenty) firms. Extensive interviews were carried out in the twenty largest accounting practices. The interviewees were either partners or managers having some responsibility for computing.

The response rates for the study are listed below. They are comparable with those reported by many other questionnaire surveys.

	Response rate (%)
Postal survey of 300 smaller accounting practices	78
Postal survey of 100 from *The Times* 1–300 companies	32
Postal survey of 100 from *The Times* 700–1000 companies	19
Postal survey of 100 from Kompass 1000–2000 companies	23
Interviews with the 20 largest accounting practices	14
Overall response rate	27.1%

The nature of the survey allowed not only analysis within each group but also the ability to contrast uses of decision support between accountants in industry and in professional practice, and between large and small practices. Full tables of results are attached at the end of this appendix.

Recent research into accountants' use of computers (Technical Change Centre, Barras and Swann 1984) suggests that accountants were very late into the field. This research suggests that computers were not seen as relevant to the traditional work of the accountant and therefore firms did not acquire machines for their own use. Where use was made of computers it tended to be bureau-based for internal administrative purposes. This stifled early development of in-house usage and expertise yet it had the benefit of not burdening the firms with large, inflexible data-processing departments. As larger accounting firms' clients moved more and more into computer systems for transactions processing and recording, the firms were forced to develop computer audit skills and facilities.

The factors mentioned above have now left the large accounting practices in a strong position. They have developed or acquired the expertise and their flexibility has enabled them to take advantage of the rapid changes in computer use.

By 1980 accounting practices seem to have dispensed with their bureau links and developed their own in-house systems. The bureaux were seen as expensive, and providing a very long turn-round time for job processing. Perhaps due to the decentralised nature of their operations, accounting firms have expressed great interest in distributed/decentralised systems. Enormous gains were felt early on from the use of word processors for such tasks as debtor circularisation. The major difficulties in computer use for accounting practices lie in the field of computer audit since clients tend to have a variety of systems in various states of competence.

A.2   Computing Facilities and Computer Types

Within the top twenty accountants considerable uniformity of equipment exists compared to the wide divergence seen in the smaller practices and in industry. However, in each there is a dominance of microcomputers over mainframes and minis. Some of the surveyed firms had mainframe facilities, but these were not used for decision support.

Two-thirds of industrial respondents used IBM mainframe, mini- or microcomputers. The number and power of the machines is a function of company size. Eleven of the major accounting firms had access to a mainframe or minicomputer for DSS purposes, only one of the smaller firms had this facility. Non-IBM work-alikes scored very poorly in all categories. Mainframe machines are oldest with the most recent moves to IBM PCs and Olivetti clones. For all sizes of firm, microcomputers now predominate. The one category where IBM does not dominate is in the smaller accounting practitioner section. Here Apricot machines are popular, followed by IBMs and its clones. A typical arrangement for these accountants is an Apricot with Supercalc software. The longer the machine has been used, the more likely it is not to be an IBM or compatible. More than half the smaller practitioners had no computer, although a number of these were actively considering acquiring one.

There is no strict correlation between small firm size and ownership of computer facilities. The mean number of partners in firms without computers was 2.17, whilst that of those practices owning machines was 11.21. However, there were firms of ten partners that posessed no hardware and a number of sole practitioners who did.

A.3   DSS Packages

Lotus 1-2-3 (a spreadsheet package) is by far the most common piece of software in the large accounting firms. Users seem to have moved to this package *en masse* just under three years ago. Smaller accounting practices have either no DSS packages or one of a number of well-known ones. The length of use of packages in this category is much smaller. Most of the smaller practitioners have used DSSs for less than eighteen months. For those who have experience of packages, Supercalc is the most common, with again a more recent move to Lotus 1-2-3. The greater variety of packages used is partially explained by the variety of machine types employed. Industrial accountants too, make most use of Lotus and Supercalc. Here there is a more substantial use of mainframe DSS packages, FCS being the dominant one. Again, there is a lack of diversity in the software used. Just eight products were mentioned by the entire sample. DSS use is clearly a function of size. The larger industrial companies had more software available and made more use of them. Mainframe modelling products have had a longer life within these firms. Most micro-based tools have appeared within the last two and a half years. Only the large accountants make use of computerised databases. Databases are a recent acquisition, the mean use time being under two years.

A.4   Uses of DSS

Budgeting is by far the most popular activity carried out by computer users in accounting functions. Industrial users also favour cashflow forecasts and consolidations although, as might be expected, accountants perform this task less. Financial planning is popular, whilst tax planning gets very little mention. Surprisingly, forecasting is a frequent activity. No other operations research technique is mentioned. It is recognised that there is some overlap in the possible activities offered to respondents and terminology may affect the answers given.

Small accounting practices tend to perform financial planning for clients to a larger extent than their bigger counterparts, perhaps reflecting a difference in clientele. Non-audit activities comprise the bulk of small accountants' workloads and this is reflected in the activities for which they use DSS. Audit planning was seldom carried out and was not thought to be particularly worthwhile.

For industrial users there is a correlation between the perceived usefulness of a system and the frequency with which it is used.

A.5   Benefits of Using DSS

Quality of output and speed are seen as the two major benefits of using a decision support system. Decision support use was not viewed as having had an effect on manpower levels. There is a tendency for the DSS user to offer new services to clients, rather than to automate or enhance existing activities. A fair degree of cynicism can be observed over the use of DSSs. The public relations and training aspects seem to dominate all others. Large accounting firms evidently do not wish to be seen lagging in the use of information technology and feel they must keep up with their clients in having knowledge of particular systems. Improving the service offered to clients was not a highly rated factor.

The training possibilities afforded by spreadsheet use was seen as a DSS benefit. Indeed, training in the use of these techniques was reported as being more valuable than actual use once learned.

It is interesting to contrast the perceived benefits of employing decision support systems in an organisation with the desirable characteristics of DSS. Users were asked to rate the usefulness of various attributes of their software. An ability to transfer files between software systems was seen as the most useful feature. Perhaps, as a result, having experienced the incompatibility of early software packages, experienced users are demanding this as a prerequisite before purchase.

Decision support users in large accounting firms thought highly of the information centre concept. Having a source of expert advice, especially if users are system builders, is seen as highly desirable. This concept is not an inherent characteristic of the software. As users explore the greater capabilities of software packages so expert advice becomes more necessary. Estimates that 80 per cent of users use only 20 per cent of system capabilities are frequently mentioned. The top twenty accounting firms may be within the other 20 percent, hence their decision to put resources into in-house information centres. This factor may have impacts on future DSS use by smaller organisations. Those without the corporate resources to sustain an information centre may find themselves never using their software to its full capabilities in case errors arise, with no help on hand. Little mention was made in this context of the software suppliers' own help facilities.

Ranked slightly below access to an information centre was the ability to tailor software packages to various requirements. Very little use was reported for local area networks or for graphics and man-machine interface attributes. The latter two factors may help explain the lack of corporate success for machines such as the Apple Macintosh, which scores well in these areas.

A.6   Users of the Systems

In all sections of the sample the builder of the system was predominantly the user. Only in a few of the larger accounting firms was there an internal modelling group. In two instances firms had a distinct policy of not allowing users to build their own models, since this was the domain of the modelling group. There are arguments both for and against this situation. These factors have been explored further in Powell (1987). Conversely, two firms saw users as eclipsing the modelling group as system builders. It may be that there is a life cycle in model building. A small core of enthusiasts become experts by building their own models. This group gives informal help to others, but users as builders predominate. A modelling group is set up, either for control or political purposes, through which all building is channelled. As other users become more expert and less satisfied with centralised model development so the modelling group is supplanted. Obviously such a life cycle is only generally applicable in any single instance. However, a correlation of the length of use of models with type of builder does offer some evidence for its existence.

Industrial firms tended to use modelling groups as system builders more than the practising accountants. Yet even here 76 per cent of the respondents claimed that the user built his own models. External consultants featured in this category, with nine firms claiming to employ them. As might be expected, only the larger companies supported an internal modelling group, though none insisted that they were the sole model builders.

It is interesting to examine the user (as opposed to the builder) group in the sample. Despite the prevailing view that computer-based models should allow expertise to flow to a lower level in the organisational hierarchy, the predominant user groups were at very senior levels. In the accounting context the output of models was used by partners, whilst the actual models were manipulated by personnel only one or two levels lower, i.e. manager/senior. In an analysis of use by levels by model types, managers were always the key users, with juniors always the least involved.

In the smaller accounting firms users were overwhelmingly at partner level. Given that a number of respondents were sole practitioners this finding was not surprising. Yet, even in larger firms where hierarchies existed, there was a clear correlation between DSS use and level in the organisation. Junior members of staff seldom used the software, whilst partners frequently did.
Industrial accountants exhibited a marked difference in the organisational levels of users. All levels were involved in model construction, although middle managers had a slightly higher usage.

As expected, those activities that traditionally occupy higher-level management, involve use of decision support by high levels in the organisation. Stategic as opposed to operational problems are the domain of top management. Thus corporate planning involves most use of DSS by partners.

Despite the much mooted move to the paperless office, there is little evidence of models being used interactively. Use of model output exceeds use of the model *in situ*. This has interesting implications from a decision standpoint. Decision makers appear to be being given outputs from the DSS without having much input to the modelling process. Thus the benefits of 'what if' and sensitivity analysis are lost if paper outputs are used. This will allow those who manipulate the model to present the decision maker with a restrictive set of outputs that could significantly alter the decision process.

A further participant in the model building process is the initiator. New models tend to be initiated by middle-ranking personnel. In the accounting context, neither partners nor audit juniors are stimulators of new modelling areas.

In the smaller accounting firms the builder and user were frequently the same individual. One respondent maintained an internal modelling group, whilst two made use of outside consultants.

In all other firms that carried out computer-based activities the user built his own systems.

A.7   Discontinued Use of DSSs

Various factors may cause a decision support tool to be abandoned. Movement from mainframe to microcomputers is an obvious reason, as was reported by several larger accounting concerns. Older micro-based tools such as Visicalc have been superseded by more sophisticated products such as Lotus. A number of products that do not fall into these categories were mentioned. Three common reasons for their demise were (1) the systems required too much internal support, and, linked to this, (2) were too complex for most users, and (3) certain products were seen as too slow and hence had been dropped. No DSS technique was reported as having been abandoned, but for most firms one or two software products fell into this category.

A.8   Future Uses

There is some similarity between the current uses listed and the future developments mentioned. Users were keenest on enhancing their ability to transfer files between applications and to generate reports, presumably in client-ready form directly from the packages. Networks rated poorly and little was thought of the use of natural language or enhancements to the man–machine interface. This may be a reflection of the fact that the interviewees were predominanly users of the output, not the system, and therefore had little interest in the software's ease of use.

The concern over file transfer was particularly mentioned in relation to clients' files. Remote auditing is seen as a future possibility with much of the audit done by transferring the client's computer files to the audit firm's machines for verification. This would go further than the current use of interrogation packages.

A.9 Expert Systems

The decision support section of this report was expressly carried out in order to gain insight into the future potential for expert systems in accounting.

The large accounting firms have for some time been exploring, to a greater or lesser extent, expert systems. However less than half the firms interviewed mentioned expert systems as a plausible future development. Those firms who have expert system development work offered a large number of potential applications. The following themes were reported:-

- An intelligent audit manual
- Expert systems for systems evaluation
- Expert systems for tax and grants advice
- Intelligent audit planning tools
- Expert systems as front-ends for computer-based training
- Artificial intelligence applied to risk assessment.

Doubts were expressed as to the ability of expert systems to deliver what they promise. The value of expert systems in the field was questioned; they were seen much more as office-based tools, used as decision aids rather than as decision makers.

As might be expected, the smaller accounting firms made no mention of expert systems as being a future development or as a current undertaking.

Interestingly, industrial firms also made no reference to expert systems either under development or as a future priority.

A.10 Other Future Intentions

The non-expert system themes which were expressed were generally in the communications area; i.e. the tying of clients' computers to those of auditors, and the ability to communicate effectively between on-site and office-based personnel. This would appear to be a move to provide more expertise to on-site staff than could be provided by phone links. Easier access to different types of hardware and compatibility between systems could be beneficial.

The future intentions of the smaller accounting firms revolved around either doing what their larger counterparts were already achieving or undertaking activities that the large firms had rejected.

The smaller firms do not suffer from the same problems posed by mainframe operating clients. There is probably more scope for undertaking decision support using microcomputers where clients are smaller. For instance, personal tax planning using adapted software packages was seen as a way forward by many small practitioners. Spreadsheets for financial planning or budgeting and staff allocation were other future intentions. There is an unrealistic element to the plans of this group. Especially evident in those practitioners who currently lacked facilities was a set of high expectations over the activities that could be easily achievable.

The future intentions of the industrial firms were for 'more of the same'. Their plans were predominantly for bigger and better systems to replace the ones currently in use. There did not appear to be a coherent information technology strategy in this group. Future intentions were *ad hoc* with little mention of coordination or consolidation of systems.

A.11 Conclusions

The survey has not produced many unexpected results; rather, it has confirmed the slow impact of computing on the accounting function. There are benefits to be gained from the use of decision support systems, yet a large number of those questioned seemed not to grasp this. The majority of small accounting firms have still not adopted computer facilities. Among those that have, standard software is not used to its fullest extent. One would expect the top twenty accounting firms to be taking the lead in this area. They appear, however, to be lead by public relations and 'keeping up with the client' motives rather than by a desire to enhance their service. These firms have seen gains arise from the adoption of new technologies but these gains are not thought to be such that any greater investment should be made. Perhaps the almost oligopolistic nature of the marketplace engenders this cautious approach. On this basis, the future for expert systems in accounting looks rather bleak. Scepticism reigns. Expert systems are a continuation of decision support systems so perhaps the firms need to feel more benefits from their current investments in IT before they will gamble on more sophisticated techniques. The current hype that surrounds expert systems has not helped. The large accounting firms have been forced into looking at expert systems so as not to be left out should their competitors embrace the technology. On the face of it accounting should provide an ideal setting for expert system development: experts abound, heuristics are employed and decisions made. Yet there is little evidence from this survey to suggest that expert systems figure significantly in accounting firms' current plans.

Table A.1 Computing facilities.

Big 20		Accountancy practices		Companies	
IBM	8	Apricot	11	IBM	73
Compaqs	7	IBM	5	Clone	5
Clones	5	Sirius	5	Olivetti	10
Macintosh	2	Compaq	3	ICL	5
Apricot	2	Tandon	2	Apricot	2
Other	2	Other	11	Macintosh	2
				Others	18
Mainframe	4		0		20
Minicomputer	7		1		12
Bureau	3		0		45

Table A.2 DSS Packages.

Big 20		Accountancy practices		Companies	
Lotus	12	Lotus	10	Lotus	31
Supercalc	4	Supercalc	20	Supercalc	19
Other	4	Multiplan	5	Symphony	12
dBASE III	3	Financial		FCS	11
RBASE	2	modelling		Insight	4
Other		systems	5	Freelance	4
databases	4	Other	7	dBASE II/III	4
File inter-		None	46	Graphwriter	3
rogation	7	None	16		
Tax	5				
Other	16				

Table A.3 The utility of DSS applications.

Rank	Big 20	Accountancy practices	Companies
1.	Budgeting	Fin. plan. (clients)	Budgeting
2.	Cash flow	Budgeting	Fin. plan.
3.	Other	Fin. plan.(internal)	Forecasting
4.	Investment appraisal	Tax planning	Cash flow
5.	Mergers & acquis'ns	Investment appraisal	Review of m'ment
6.	Financial planning	Analytic review	Corporate planning
7.	Corporate planning	Audit management	Mergers & acquis'ns
8.	Tax planning	Audit planning	Investment appraisal

Table A.4 The benefits of using DSS for the large accounting firms. (on a scale of 0−5)

Reason	Mean	Standard deviation
Quality	3.06	0.36
Reduced manpower	1.66	0.73
Speed	3.15	0.58
PR with clients	5 firms	
Training of staff	5 "	
Improve services to clients	3 "	
Improve staff morale	2 "	

Table A.5 Future intentions (big 20 = 14 firms)

1.	Audit planning	8
2.	Expert systems	6
3.	Tax	5
4.	Database developments	5
5.	Automated checklists	4
6.	Analytic review	3
7.	Statistical analysis	3
8.	Budgeting	2
9.	Risk analysis	2
10.	Investment appraisal	1

Table A.6 Important future
developments (big 20 = 14 firms)

Expert systems	8
Audit judgement and planning:	
Control evaluation	5
Tax	2
Non-tax regulations	1
Accounts presentation	1
Computerised methodology	1
Training	1
Input to areas of staff scheduling in audit planning using M.P.	1
Non-expert systems	
Communications	9
Hardware/software improvements	6
Other	5
Audit project planning	3
Accounts preparation	3
Other	5

Table A.7 Future intentions
(smaller firms, non-big 20)

Tax	9
Spreadsheet	9
Budgeting	7
Financial planning	7
Cash flow	3
Audit planning	2
Integrated office systems	2
Other	7

Table A.8 Future intentions (companies)

Investment appraisal	3
Database	3
Budgeting	3
Cash flow	3
Forecasting	3
Treasury	2
Integrating systems	2
Financial planning	2
Mergers and acquisitions	2
Other	6

Appendix B

The Preliminary Survey

B.1 Introduction

The purpose of the survey was assess the level of involvement of accounting professionals in the development of expert systems, their estimate of the worth of expert systems, and their intentions for future involvement in expert systems development.

The survey was executed in two phases. The initial phase, the preliminary survey, was designed to establish which firms were involved in expert systems to any significant degree. Having processed the preliminary survey results a detailed questionnaire was then sent to those respondents who seemed to have a substantial involvement in expert systems development. The results of the detailed questionnaire are presented in Appendix C.

Of the 600 preliminary questionnaires sent out 188 replies were received giving a response of 31.3 per cent. Differences between three geographical locations and professional categories were considered. Information was elicited through asking the following questions:

(1) 'Are you involved in expert systems development?'
(2) 'How many employees do you have?'
(3) 'If you are not involved then why not?'
(4) 'If so, to what degree?'
(5)   to what extent?'
(6)   using which tools?'
(7)   using a developed methodology?'
(8)   in which application areas?'

The following codes were used:

The United Kingdom	UK
The United States	US
Canada	CA
Accounting firms	AA
Industrial companies	CC
Finance houses	FH
Non-life insurance	IN
Life insurance	IL

The sample

Six hundred preliminary survey questionnaires were dispatched during the summer of 1986 to three geographical and two main professional categories. The geographical categories were the UK, the US and Canada. The questionnaires were addressed, in the main, either to individual offices of accounting firms or to the accounting departments of large industrial companies. The UK part of the sample also contained some representatives of finance houses and the insurance business.

The questionnaires were sent only to the largest firms in the UK, since it was felt that smaller firms were unlikely to be involved in expert systems development to any significant degree.

In terms of geographical and professional categories the distribution of the sample is represented in the table below.

Sample distribution (percentages of total sample; actual numbers of respondents in parentheses)

	UK %	US	CA	Total
AA	11 (21)	18 (34)	16 (31)	46 (86)
CC	21 (40)	12 (23)	—	34 (64)
FH	6 (11)	—	—	
IL	6 (11)	—	—	
IN	9 (17)	—	—	
Total	53 (100)	30 (57)	16 (31)	100 (188)

Comments

Our selection of geographical and professional categories was influenced by two principal areas of interest: first, whether the US was ahead of the UK in expert systems development in accounting, and second, how the accounting community was reacting to the emergence of knowledge-based systems as a viable and useful technology. The sample is restricted to members and affiliates of the Institute mainly in the US and the UK. However, it was felt that it would be useful to include in the sample some Canadian accounting offices in order to give an indication of their level of expert systems awareness. Also, it was considered important not to limit the survey to members in accountancy firms but to include accountants employed in industry as well. However, there is no industrial company data for Canada, as it was felt that for the purpose of our transatlantic comparison sufficient information could be derived from UK and US companies.

Our preliminary investigations had indicated a high level of awareness by UK insurance and finance houses. Representatives of these institutions are therefore included within the survey although the sample sizes are very small and the results should therefore be interpreted in this light.

B.2   Preliminary Survey Results

(1) 'Are you involved in expert systems development?'

Table B.1 gives the percentage of respondents in each category who answered 'yes'. 'Union' indicates groupings of respondent firms which include more than one country or more than one professional category.

Table B.1 Involvement in ES development (%)

	UK	US	CA	Union
AA	48	53	39	47
CC	55	61	—	58
FH	36	—	—	
IL	36	—	—	
IN	53	—	—	
Union	49	56	39	50

Comments

(a) Both UK and US data indicate that industrial companies are more involved in expert systems development than accounting firms.

(b) Canadian involvement appears to trail some way behind that in the US and the UK. However, it should be noted that there is no company (CC) data for Canada, which probably would have contributed to a higher total figure given comment (a).

(c) The UK data suggest that non-life insurance companies are more involved than either life insurance or finance houses, but only slightly if the 3 to 2 respondent ratio is allowed for.

(2) 'How many employees do you have?'

Table B.2 shows the mean employee count for sample classes who are and who are not involved in expert systems development.

Table B.2

	Involved	Not involved
UK AA	2500	700
UK CC	3100	3800
UK FH	240	200
UK IL	260	2600
UK IN	2600	2600
US AA	1400	370
US CC	1900	1300
CA AA	400	1000
All UK	2300	2600
All US	1600	700
All CA	400	1000
All AA	1300	600
All CC	2700	3000
Total	1700	1800

Comment

(a) Ignoring the groups with small samples, the only information that can be derived from Table B.2 is that the involved accounting firms tend to be the large ones, whereas the company data are much more ambivalent.

(3) 'If you are not involved then why not?'

Table B.3 gives the percentage of respondents in each category who answered 'no' to question (1).

Table B.3

	Benefits unclear	No trained staff	Other commit- ments	Tools too primitive
UK AA	64	27	64	0
UK CC	67	11	67	17
UK FH	43	14	71	0
UK IL	100	14	29	0
UK IN	88	12	38	25
US AA	62	50	44	19
US CC	44	33	78	44
CA AA	47	68	37	21
All UK	71	16	57	10
All US	56	44	56	28
All CA	47	68	37	21
All AA	57	52	46	15
All CC	59	19	70	26
Total	62	34	53	17

Comments

(a) Overall, of those respondents who were not involved in expert systems development, 62 per cent thought that the benefits of the new technology were unclear, 53 per cent said that they had more pressing developments to attend to, 34 per cent had insufficiently trained staff and 17 per cent thought the tools were too primitive.

(b) The major difference between accounting firms and industrial companies was that the great majority of industrial companies did not feel that they lacked trained staff whereas half the accounting firms did.

(c) Doubts with respect to benefits are greater in the UK than in North America, but a much smaller proportion of UK respondents indicated that they lacked suitably trained staff. An important question is to what degree is the lack of awareness of benefits connected with the lack of awareness of staff requirements. It could be that the Americans, with fewer doubts as to benefits, have a better idea about staff requirements.

(d) Comparison of US accounting and industrial companies reveals that accounting firms harbour more doubts (62 per cent) than industrial companies (44 per cent). This pattern is not repeated in the corresponding UK data (64 per cent vs 67 per cent). An equally marked US–UK difference appears when comparing the commitment to other projects by firms and companies. Figures for the US are 44 per cent and 78 per cent compared with 64 per cent and 67 per cent for the UK. It would seem that accountants in US companies are more aware (than other groups) of the benefits of expert systems even though they consider themselves too committed to other projects to invest in expert systems developments. Have these companies dismissed the exploitation of expert systems as commercially viable? To what extent does cross fertilisation take place between accountants and other company departments who are building non-accounting expert systems?

(4) 'To what degree are you active in expert systems development?'

Table B.4 gives the percentages of respondents in each category who answered 'yes' to question (1) (see also Figures B.1 and B.2).

Table B.4

	Unofficial champion	Official champion	Several part-timers	Large group	Major dept
UK AA	30	40	20	10	0
UK CC	41	23	14	9	5
UK FH	0	0	50	0	0
UK IL	0	50	0	0	0
UK IN	33	11	22	11	22
US AA	28	17	11	6	11
US CC	21	7	14	21	29
CA AA	42	58	17	8	8
All UK	31	24	18	8	6
All US	25	12	12	12	19
All CA	42	58	17	8	8
All AA	32	35	15	8	8
All CC	33	17	14	14	14
Total	30	25	16	10	11

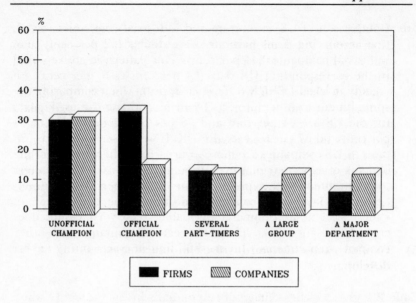

Figure B.1   Degree of involvement - firms vs companies

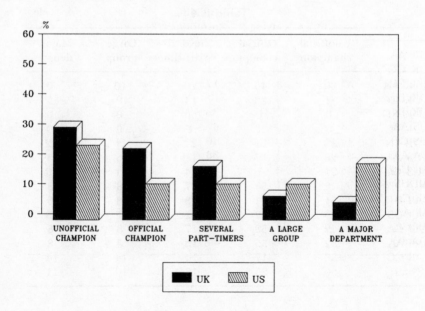

Figure B.2   Degree of involvement - UK vs US

Comments

(a) Expert systems technology is evidently still in its formative years since it is still largely the responsibility of individual champions, official or unofficial.

(b) Accounting firms tend to have more official champions than industrial companies, but the latter have more large official groups and major departments.

(c) The US is more involved than the UK or Canada.

(d) It is noteworthy that as many as 29 per cent of US industrial companies assert that they have a major department dedicated to the exploitation of expert systems. The corresponding figure (22 per cent) of British non-life insurance is also large.

(5) 'To what extent are you involved in expert systems development?'

Table B.5 gives the percentage of respondents in each category who answered 'yes' to question (1) (see also Figures B.3–B.6).

Table B.5

	Reading	Playing	Building prototypes	Building full-scale systems	Using full-scale systems
UK AA	40	33	40	20	13
UK CC	32	36	41	27	27
UK FH	33	33	17	17	33
UK IL	25	50	0	0	0
UK IN	56	22	33	44	33
US AA	58	53	47	37	32
US CC	40	40	40	47	33
CA AA	54	46	38	31	8
All UK	38	34	34	25	23
All US	50	47	44	41	32
All CA	54	46	38	31	8
All AA	51	45	43	30	19
All CC	35	38	41	35	30
Total	44	40	38	31	24

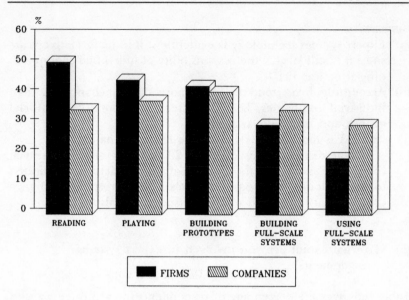

Figure B.3 Extent of involvement - firms vs companies.

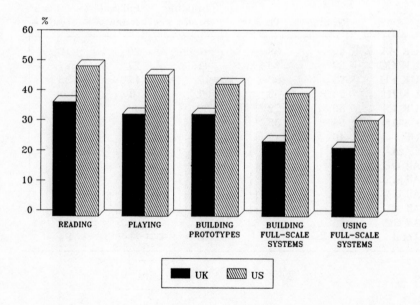

Figure B.4 Extent of involvement - UK vs US

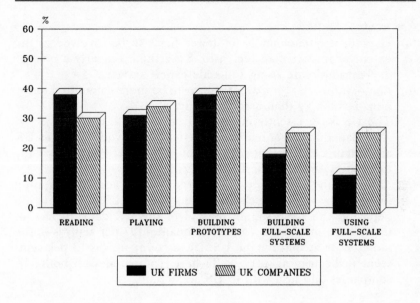

Figure B.5 Extent of involvement - UK firms vs companies

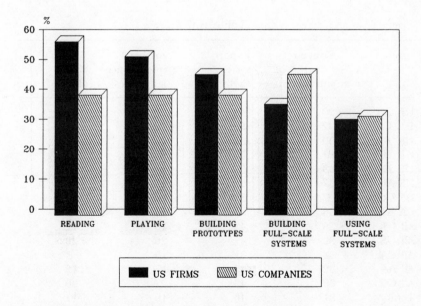

Figure B.6 Extent of involvement - US firms vs companies

Comments

(a) Overall, the tendency is for fewer firms to be involved as the extent of involvement increases. Nevertheless, nearly a quarter of the sample are using full-scale expert systems.
(b) Again, industrial companies appear to be more committed to the new technology than accounting firms.
(c) The US is consistently more involved than the UK.
(d) The Canadian accountants are at least as involved as the UK accountants except that they do not profess to be using as many full-scale systems as the British.
(e) Although the proportion (32 per cent) of US accountants using full-scale systems is much the same as that of US companies (33 per cent) the same cannot be said of the UK data. In fact although the proportion for UK companies (27 per cent) is of the same order as that for the US, UK accountants (at 13 per cent) seem to be lagging very badly here, compared with both UK companies and also with to US accountants.

(6) 'What tools are you using?'

Table B.6 gives the percentage of respondents in each category who answered 'yes' to question (1) (see also Figures B.7 and B.8).

Table B.6

	Conven- tional software	Expert system shells	Artificial intelligence languages	Tool kits
UK AA	20	47	20	13
UK CC	32	50	18	18
UK FH	50	33	0	17
UK IL	0	50	25	0
UK IN	33	56	11	0
US AA	37	58	16	16
US CC	27	33	40	47
CA AA	38	31	15	8
All UK	29	48	16	12
All US	32	47	26	29
All CA	38	31	15	8
All AA	32	47	17	13
All CC	30	43	27	30
Total	31	46	19	17

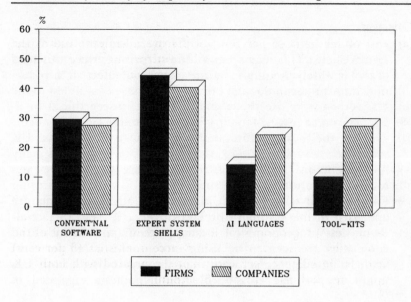

Figure B.7 Tools used - firms vs companies

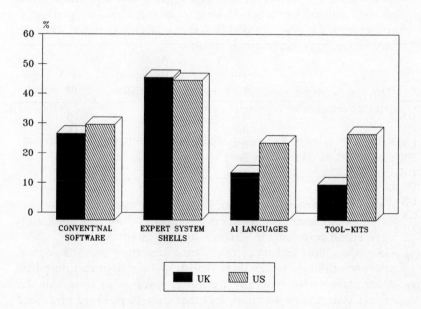

Figure B.8 Tools used - UK vs US

Comments

(a) Just under half (46 per cent) of the overall sample use expert system shells. This may seem a little surprising, since this kind of tool is widely thought to be an ideal way to effect an introduction into the technology.

(b) UK respondents use shells more than they use artificial intelligence languages and tool-kits, in contrast to the US respondents who use the more sophisticated software to a much higher degree.

(c) Accountants in US industrial companies use AI languages and tool-kits more than they do shells.

(d) From (b) and (c) we might infer a more advanced or mature approach in the US than in the UK.

(e) Regardless of geographical location, accountants in industrial companies are seen to be using more sophisticated forms of artificial intelligence software than the accounting firms. This might support the cross-fertilisation hypothesis suggested in (3)(d).

(f) The use of conventional software (31 per cent of the sample) may be a reflection of the perceived state of tools available. Alternatively, a blurred distinction between traditional decision support systems and expert systems may have led to the inclusion of some of the former in this figure. Alternatively, the absence of staff trained in use of AI languages and tools, coupled with the presence of staff trained in the use of conventional software languages, may explain this result.

(7) 'Do you have an established methodology for the development of expert systems?'

Table B.7 gives the percentage of the sub-group that replied affirmatively to question (1).

Comments

(a) A significant proportion (23 per cent) of the sample indicate that they have an established expert systems development methodology. These respondents warrant further attention.

(b) US respondents feel more confident about their methodological approach than do either their British or Canadian counterparts.

(c) Accountants, who generally are not as involved as companies in expert systems construction, feel that they have more of a hold on the methodological issues. This would appear to be a strange finding indeed and particularly so for the UK accountants who have the least experience of all and of whom 30 per cent profess to having an established methodology. This result might reflect the accountant's traditional professional involvement with methodological issues.

Table B.7

UK AA	UK CC	UK FH	UK IL	UK NL	US AA	US CC	CA AA	All UK	All US	All CA	All AA	All CC	Total
30	14	25	0	22	33	29	17	18	31	17	28	19	23

(8) 'In what application areas are you developing expert systems?'

Table B.8 gives the actual numbers of applications within each area.

Comments
(a) The categorisation of responses has been made more difficult by the wide spread of applications and by the vagueness of some of their titles, which may make extrapolation unwise.
(b) A clear distinction was expected between the responses from accountancy firms and those practising in industry. However, the ratio of accounting to non-accounting applications within industry is more marked than might have been expected. This is particularly so in the responses from American companies, leading to a disproportionate representation of systems in the 'other' category.
(c) In accountancy firms, design and planning of the audit featured strongly. It seems surprising that taxation systems were poorly represented.
(d) It seems likely that many systems are small and little more than experimental — an hypothesis that will be tested by an examination of the responses to the detailed questionnaire.

Table B.8

Applications	UK AA	UK CC	UK FH	UK IL	UK NL	US AA	US CC	CA AA	Totals
Audit									
Audit (general)	1					2			3
Analytical review	2					1			3
Audit risk							1		1
Companies Act Compliance	1								1
Design of audit programme	3					6			9
Evaluation of controls	1								1
Going concern						1			1
Materiality							1		1
Sampling						1			1
Sources of audit satisfaction							1		1
Tax accrual and planning	1								1
									23
Taxation									
Directors' transactions	2								2
Personal financial planning		1				1		1	3
Tax	2					3			5
									10
Data Processing									
DP audit planning	3								3
DP performance	4	2							6
Software evaluation	1							1	2
									11
Other Financial									
Acquisition Analysis		1							1
Financial analysis	1			1	1		1		4
									5
General Business									
Admin							1	1	2
Business modelling		4	3		1	1		1	10
Consulting						2			2
Employment law	1								1
Forecasting		1	2		2				5
Recruitment and personnel	1	1							2
Underwriting				1	4				5
									27
Others	2	5	6	1	8	8	16	1	47
Total	26	15	11	3	16	26	18	8	123

Appendix C

The Detailed Survey

Introduction

Although some 45 of the 189 respondents to the preliminary questionnaire indicated that they would be willing to reply to the detailed questionnaire, only twelve completed detailed questionnaires were returned. The reason provided by those firms who belatedly declined to complete the detailed questionnaire was that they realised that they were not as involved in the area as they at had first thought. No doubt this reaction was precipitated largely by the size and detailed nature of the questionnaire once it arrived. It may also be the case that some firms felt that the information requested was of too confidential a nature. This appendix provides a summary of those completed scripts that were returned.

The questionnaire was structured in five parts as follows:

Part 1: General objectives covered the reasons for the organisation's interest in expert systems, the origin of this interest, the length of time involved in expert systems development and the expected financial return on the developmental investment made.

Part 2 addressed the *current level of involvement* in terms of current usage, manpower investment, monetary investment, the hardware and software tools used, and the application areas addressed.

Part 3 addressed the *technical issues* associated with the respondent's most complex system.

Part 4 investigated the organisation's likely *future involvement* in
expert systems in terms of the extent and level of their predicted use
and the areas in which they were likely to be used.

Part 5 sought estimates of the *likely impact* of expert systems on
accounting in terms of their level and scope of use.

This report covers the material found in the twelve completed
scripts returned (and not all of these were entirely completed).
Clearly, the sample was too small to provide statistically meaningful
results so only a descriptive summary of the responses has been
attempted. The numbers in parentheses indicate how many of the
respondents agreed with a particular statement.

Half of the twelve replies were from the UK and the rest were
from the US and Canada. All of the replies came from accounting
firms.

Part 1: General Objectives

O The principal reason for a firm being involved in expert systems
was to broaden its services to clients or client departments (10). This
reason was closely followed by a desire to keep abreast of technological change (8) and a desire to keep abreast or ahead of competitors
(8).
O In general, the requirement for expert systems development had
come from an internal department or group (9).
O The firms had been aware of expert systems for between two
to five years (9) and had begun developing their own systems between 1983 and 1985 (9).
O A small proportion of the sample (3 out of 12) stated that they
had already obtained a financial return on expert systems development and the same proportion expected a return in two to four
years.
O When the expected return was considered estimable, most of the
respondents thought that it would be in the region of 2:1.

Part 2: The Current Level of Involvement

O Almost all of the respondents stated that expert systems were currently being developed as experimental prototypes (11) and for only a few were expert systems in regular use as operational business systems (3), or on a trial basis (3), or being developed as products (2).
O The number of people involved in full-time expert systems research and development varied between 0.5 and 6, with a mean at 2.8.
O Budgetary information was largely confidential but investment levels of 5–10 per cent of the research and development budget were typical of those who did reply.
O By far the most quoted hardware were the IBM PC, XT and AT (or look-alikes) and the most quoted shell was Xi (6). The shells Expert Ease (2), APES (2), ES/P Advisor (2), Expert Edge (3), CRYSTAL (2) and M.1. (2) were also mentioned.

The *application areas* mentioned by the respondents were:

- Audit planning
- Audit software advice
- Business expansion
- Checklist generator (for financial statements requirements)
- Computer-assisted audit technique choice
- Computer audit risk identification
- Directors' transactions (legality of)
- Employment law
- Financial statements analysis
- Going concern judgement
- Government grants (applicability of)
- Graduate recruitment
- Personal financial planning
- Project risk assessment
- Sales analysis
- Substantive test programme generation
- Tax accrual and planning

The *criteria* used for the selection of these tasks for expert systems application areas were of two types. First, there were 'problem-led' criteria for which the awareness of a problem led to the attempt at an expert system approach for its solution, and second, 'solution-led' criteria for which it had been decided to use expert systems purely in order to gain experience in their use. There follows a summary of these criteria.

Problem-led criteria
* identified by potential users
* existing documentation needed updating
* need for internal standards/consistency
* task excessively time consuming
* shortage of personnel to do task
* task was in a critical business area

Solution-led criteria
* domain was complex but formal
* identified by DP department–audit group committee
* domain was narrow
* domain was well bounded

The *anticipated benefits* included
* education and greater awareness/experience
* greater efficiency
* greater effectiveness
* standardisation of/consistency in company practices
* distribution of company expertise
* improvement of company expertise
* commercial return
* public relations for firm
* shell evaluation
* reduction in costs
* training spin-off

The *performance criteria* included
* accuracy
* ease of use
* soundness/competence
* ease of maintenance
* speed of response

The *criteria for success* mentioned were:
* user acceptability
* ease and clarity of use
* efficiency
* financial breakeven
* improvement in product quality

- decrease in product cost
- useful research
- stimulation of in-house interest
- widespread use

The *status of the systems* described were about evenly divided between 'prototype', 'trial' and 'fully operational'.

Part 3: Technical Issues

Only six respondents replied to this part describing implemented systems so the data are very sparse. However, there follows a summary of significant points not addressed by part 2.

O The functions addressed by the systems described included elements of interpretation, diagnosis and planning. The number of rules varied between 200 and 5000.

O Five of the systems were implemented using shells (ESP/ADVISOR, CRYSTAL, TESS, Xi, AION ADS), the remaining one being implemented in Golden Common LISP.

O The hardware chosen was always an IBM PC (XT or AT).

O The systems were generally of the consultative stand-alone type although three accessed external files.

O Five of the six systems used production rules as the method of knowledge representation. The remaining one used frames.

O The knowledge representation method used was determined either by the nature of the software used or because it seemed the most appropriate method for the problem chosen.

O All the systems used backward chaining as an inference strategy. Three used forward chaining as well.

O The systems generally used crisp logic but some incorporated uncertainty as well.

O Explanation and justification was generally mediated via rule tracing. On-line help was also generally available.

O It was generally found that a conventional approach to software development was not appropriate for the construction of expert systems.

O All of the development cycles discussed involved a prototyping element. A typical development cycle follows:

- Identification of Domain
- Review of Domain Literature
- Definition of Problem
- Selection of Expert
- Initial Interview with Expert
- Choice of Shell or Software
- Partial Systems Analysis
- Prototype Construction
  - Knowledge Elicitation
  - System Design
  - System Implementation
  - System Demonstration/Testing
  - Calibration/Refinement
- Review of Lessons Learned
- Implementation of Final System
- User System Testing

O System development was generally controlled by regular reviews by systems builders, experts, users, and managers.
O Documentation was generally very informal and there was no consensus as to what constituted appropriate documents.
O The most frequently mentioned source of knowledge was an expert.
O Knowledge engineers working in conjunction with experts were used as frequently as experts working alone to produce a system.
O The experts were generally members of the firm producing the system.
O Case study inspection was the most quoted approach to testing.
O By and large the systems could be maintained by relatively computer-naive people.
O Formal testing procedures were practised by a majority of the firms.
O The benefits predicted for the systems were generally matched by their performance.
O The degree to which the systems were finally used was varied.

The lessons learned during the projects included the following:

O More effort should have been expended in persuading the user community of the benefits of expert systems.
O Expert systems need to be integrated with existing data-processing systems.
O The chosen application domain should not be subject to rapid change.

O   The chosen project/task should be small in the first instance.
O   Final hardware/software decisions should be put off until the final design stage.
O   Formal external knowledge engineering training would have been appropriate.

The key decisions leading to a successful outcome were:
O   well-considered problem identification
O   matching the problem chosen with the perceived benefits
O   not being over-ambitious
O   listening closely to the users requirements
O   using only one expert
O   having a credible expert who communicated well
O   attempting to build an expert assistant rather than an expert replacement
O   prototyping, i.e. not trying to analyse the task to death at an early stage
O   inputting rules directly
O   encouraging close contact between the knowledge engineer and the expert

Part 4: Likely Future Involvement

O   The most likely areas of future development were considered to be audit procedures/testing, audit planning and personal taxation, followed closely by corporate taxation, financial planning, management advisory services and training.
O   The criteria used in coming to the above judgements were largely based on perceived organisational needs and knowledge of current corporate plans on the one hand, and the nature of the areas involved on the other.
O   Availability of appropriate hardware was not thought likely to be a constraint on expert systems development. This was also true of software but to a slightly lesser degree.
O   It was generally thought, however, that lack of suitably trained personnel might be a problem in the future.

It was anticipated that the most likely users of expert systems would be ranked in the following order:

- managers
- supervisors
- partners
- trainees
- newly qualified staff
- clients

By and large, the most acceptable user interface facilities were likely to include the keyboard, menus, and multiple-window displays (with roughly equivalent weight).

Part 5: The Likely Impact of Expert Systems on Accounting

O It was generally agreed that expert systems are likely to have a limited impact in a variety of areas by the end of 1988, a significant impact in a few areas by the end of 1990, and a significant impact in a variety of areas by the end of 1994.

O It was thought that expert systems will have their greatest impact in the areas of personal taxation, corporate taxation and financial planning, closely followed by capital project planning, audit procedures/testing, audit planning and training.

O Respondents thought that the forms that the impact would take were more likely be the performance of existing tasks more efficiently and the overcoming of skills shortages than the performance of new tasks.

O The main constraints to the future development of expert systems in accountancy were seen as:
- lack of internal financial commitment
- lack of time
- lack of skills
- lack of user acceptance
- non-availability of experts
- lack of domain-specific shells
- disenchantment with current levels of achievement

O Few of the respondents' clients have involved them in the development of expert systems to date, but it was thought that the most likely areas of future involvement with clients would be through expert systems related consultancy and the auditing of a client's expert systems. It was generally believed that the development of financial expert systems would have no significant effect on the respondents' relationships with their clients.

O   All of the respondents reported that they were considering the effect that expert systems will have on their auditing/accounting practices.

Conclusion

The overall view provided by this survey, sparse though the data sometimes are, is of a community that is still in the very early stages of learning how to exploit a new technology. There is a degree of scepticism concerning, not so much the benefits of expert systems, but rather whether the promise of their implementation can be fulfilled at all. There is also a corresponding hesitancy in committing resources for expert systems development. However there has been some considerable effort, on the part of one or two firms, towards the implementation of such systems. In these cases this effort seems to have been rewarded, by and large, by an increased awareness of the specific problem areas surrounding the technology and of the directions in which research and development should move in order to solve those problems. For those firms that have taken these development risks there also appears to be a growing confidence of the reality of the ultimate utility and power of developing knowledge-based approaches to problem solving.

Appendix D

The Question Form

Script References:

_____

_____

_____

Area	Phases	Contexts
change control	specification	agent
_____	_____	_____
_____	_____	_____
_____	_____	_____

Question Name: q_user_specification

Question: Do users participate throughout the amendment specification process?

Q U E S T I O N   F O R M (page 2)

Explanation: (I am asking this question because ...)

For any system to be developed successfully it is very important that the user of that system is involved in specifying exactly what it is that he requires and then in ensuring that his specifications are being met throughout the development process.

Answer Range:

1. Yes

2. No

3. _____

4. _____

5. _____

Risks: (The specific consequences associated with these possible answers are:)

1. (no risks)   _____

    _____

2. There is a higher risk of specification error.   _____

    _____

3. _____

    _____

QUESTION FORM   (page 3)

4. _____

   _____

5. _____

   _____

Contributes to which control objectives/sub-objectives:

This question provides information that contributes to the
evaluation of the following goals:

user-involvement   _____

specification-error   _____

user-satisfaction   _____

likelihood-of-unauthorised-amendment   _____

statutory-amendment-error   _____

_____

_____

_____

QUESTION FORM (page 4)

Is relevant to which interviewee classes:

Senior management [x]

User [x]

Development and support [x]

Operations [x]

User support [ ]

Administration [ ]

Is constrained by company profile values as follows:

(not constrained) _____

_____

_____

_____

Is constrained by review objective values as follows:

(not constrained) _____

_____

_____

_____

QUESTION FORM   (page 5)

Other constraints:

_____

_____

_____

_____

_____

_____

_____

QUESTION FORM   (page 6)

Any Other Comments:

_____

_____

_____

_____

_____

_____

_____

Appendix E

The System Specification

E.1 Introduction

The knowledge base focuses, as stated, upon Section 4.4 of the overall review area — the software access controls section of the sub-area physical security and logical access controls. In particular, the knowledge centres around a network of fifteen IBM System 34 specific questions and a further eighteen general questions which are used when it is not known what machine/configuration is being used at the installation being reviewed. The expertise manifests itself in two ways: first in knowing which questions to ask, and second, in knowing how to evaluate the answers. For convenience, the questions are listed below together with labels which will be referred to in later sections where the relationships between them are discussed. It is also convenient to list the explanation text together with the corresponding question. Questions are indicated by Q and explanations by E.

E.2 The General Questions

Label	Questions and explanations
q44aiA	Q Is the operating system (or an additional access control package) capable of enforcing segregation of duties by restricting access to the computer system?
	E If there is not software facility for restricting access to the computer system the consequences from the

point of view of program and data security would probably be very serious.

q44aiB Q Are the facilities offered by the operating system for restricting access to the computer system used?

   E Even if there is a facility for restricting access to the computer system, its use should be checked in any assessment of the quality of the access controls.

q44aii1A Q Is the operating system (or an additional access control package) capable of enforcing segregation of duties by restricting user access to particular terminals?

   E Limited access to terminals is a useful way of enforcing segregation of duties.

q44aii1B Q Are the facilities, offered by the operating system or additional access control software security package, for restricting user access to particular terminals being used?

   E Restricting user access to terminals is one way of enhancing segregation of duties control.

q44aii2A Q Is the operating system (or additional access control package) capable of enforcing segregation of duties by restricting user access to particular menus or options within menus?

   E An absence of sign-on security would leave a system extremely vulnerable.

q44aii2B Q Are the facilities, offered by the operating system or additional access control software security package, for restricting user access to particular menus or options within menus being used?

   E Log-on security is extremely important in a computer environment in which many people work.

q44aii3A Q Is the operating system (or an additional access control package) capable of enforcing segregation of duties by restricting user access to particular programs?

   E Users must be restricted from completely free access to programs in order to minimise the possibility of unauthorised amendments and therefore of error and fraud.

q44aii3B   Q   Are the facilities, offered by the operating system or additional access control software security package, for restricting user access to particular programs being used?

            E   Programs should be protected against unauthorised access, the danger here being the risk of error and fraud.

q44aii4A   Q   Is the operating system (or an additional access control package) capable of enforcing segregation of duties by restricting user access to particular data files?

            E   Corruption of data can cause problems. Restricting personnel access to it can therefore reduce this danger.

q44aii4B   Q   Are the facilities, offered by the operating system or additional access control software security package, for restricting user access to particular data files being used?

            E   Data files, like programs, should be protected against the unauthorised meddler.

q44bi   Q   Does the access control facility lock-out repeated attempts to log on after, say, three unsuccessful attempts?

            E   Locking out persistently unsuccessful attempts to log on is a fairly basic control against hacking. If the attempts are logged, then so much the better.

q44bii   Q   Does the access control facility time-out terminals that have been logged on but have remained inactive for a predetermined period of time?

            E   This feature is a control against someone leaving their terminal and forgetting that they left it on.

q44biii   Q   Does the access control facility prevent a user from logging on to more than one terminal at a time?

            E   (no explanation)

q44biv   Q   Does the access control facility restrict the reporting
                of passwords and security tables to authorised
                persons?
            E   Knowledge of passwords should clearly be restricted
                to those authorised to use them.

q44c   Q   Where appropriate, is the password control that is
                available at operating system level supplemented
                by additional password controls within individual
                applications?
            E   If operating system level password constraints are
                reinforced by application program password con-
                straints then so much the better for limiting the
                possibility of unauthorised access to information.

q44di   Q   Are all unsuccessful attempts to log on or input
                restricted transaction types logged by the system and
                reported directly to an on-line security terminal
                and/or subsequently printed out in the form or a
                security exception report?
            E   This is a facility which could form a detective
                control on unauthorised access to information.

q44dii   Q   Are there adequate procedures for the review and,
                where necessary, the investigation of these reports?
            E   Effecting a detective control over possibly unauthor-
                ised attempts at logging on to the system.

q44e   Q   Are software house representatives restricted to
                accessing the computer via a test environment?
            E   If a consulting software house is not restricted to
                doing its testing, etc., via a test environment then
                it might gain access to sensitive information.

E.3 The IBM System 34 Questions

Label   *Questions and explanations*

q44za1a   Q   Is sign-on security used for all users?
            E<insert Glossary 'sign on security' text>

q44za1b1a Q Has the client written his own access control package?

E We are trying to find out if there are any compensating controls for the fact that sign-on security is not used. Should the user answer 'yes' to this question then it will be suggested to him that he should really be involved in the non-IBM System 34 line of questioning and should go to the beginning and alter the general details appropriately.

q44za1b1b Q Has a third-party software access control system been purchased?

E We are trying to find out if there are any compensating controls for the fact that sign-on security is not used. Should the user answer 'yes' to this question then it will be suggested to him that he should really be involved in the non-IBM system 34 line of questioning and should go to the beginning and alter the general details appropriately.

q44za1b2 Q Is physical access to terminals restricted in such a way as to promote a segregation of duties?

E In this case sign-on is not being used, and no alternative access control system is being used, so we are interested in finding out whether there are physical access controls that can compensate for the above lack of software access controls. Even if the answer to this question is 'yes' it will have been established that the access controls are poor. If the user answers 'no', then the expert's opinion is that it is not worth asking any more questions about software access security since they are so poor that any further questioning could not possibly lead to an improved assessment.

q44za2a Q Is menu security used?

E Sign-on is probably sufficient to restrict access to the computer system to employees, but we still have to find out if the logical access controls are sufficient to enforce a segregation of functions.

q44za2b Q Are all users, including computer operators, restricted to only those facilities they require for the performance of their duties by the use of mandatory menus?

E   Just because menu security is used there is no guarantee that it enforces segregation of functions. Therefore this question must be asked.

q44za2c1   Q   Have the System 34 resource security facilities been established to enforce an appropriate segregation of functions?

E   Two types of access control are desirable: (1) menu security, and (2) resource security. Ideally both should be used but in certain circumstances it could be appropriate to use either. Therefore, since menu security is not used we are trying to find out if resource security compensates for the lack of use of menu security.

q44za2c2a   Q   Is access to individual applications restricted by the use of application-specific passwords?

E   We are trying to find a compensating control for the lack of menu and resource security. Application packages are frequently supplied with some kind of in-built password security.

q44za2c2b   Q   Are the passwords used to restrict access to specific applications capable of enforcing an appropriate segregation of functions?

E   We have ascertained that at this computer installation the client has not made use of the IBM System 34 standard access control features (resource and menu security), however we have identified that software access control is being provided as part of the application programs in the form of passwords. We are here attempting to find out if these are appropriate to enforce a segregation of functions.

q44za2c3a   Q   Is access to the applications controlled by non--System 34 access control software?

E   At this stage we know that there is no menu security, no resource security and no controls within the applications so we are still trying to find suitable compensating controls.

q44za2c3b   Q   Is this appropriate to enforce the segregation of functions?

E   (Please use the Glossary for an explanation of segregation of functions.)

q44za2c4   Q   Are the terminals so located that users are subject to continual supervision so that any unauthorised use of the computer system would be detected and prevented?

E   We have a situation in which there are no software controls to enforce a segregation of functions so we are left with investigating whether there are raw physical controls which will serve this purpose.

q44za3a   Q   Is the resource security used to protect access to sensitive program libraries and data files?

E   <insert Glossary 'resource security' text>

q44za3b   Q   Considering that resource security is not used, are there any compensating procedures to protect sensitive program files and libraries?

E   (no explanation)

q44za4   Q   Is access to sensitive functions or resources further restricted by the use of application specific passwords?

E   This question serves to enhance the quality of the controls investigated.

E.4   Constraints on Question Answering

It was found that the expert's initial concerns were with fact gathering as well as with the direct assessment of the controls. Thus there is a separation between two kinds of knowledge articulated by the experts — knowing which question to ask next, and knowing how to evaluate the answers. The first aspect of the experts' knowledge is represented here (although it is not possible to completely separate out the two kinds of knowledge). The questions are presented in their order of articulation along with any conditions that constrain their use. A question may take one of three answered values: Y (yes), N (no), or U (unknown). If an assertion has not yet been evaluated it

will have a value of 'unanswered' which is represented by ~A. ~Y
is taken to mean either N or U.

(a) Question constraints: The general questions

Question	Constraint	Question	Constraint
q44aiA		q44aii4B	q44aii4A = Y
q44aiB	q44aiA = Y	q44bi	
q44aii1A		q44bii	
q44aii1B	q44aii1A = Y	q44biii	
q44aii2A		q44biv	
q44aii2B	q44aii2A = Y	q44c	
q44aii3A		q44di	
q44aii3B	q44aii3A = Y	q44dii	
q44aii4A		q44e	

(b)   Question constraints: The IBM System 34 questions

The situation with the IBM System 34 questions is rather more
complicated in that the expert concerned defined sub-issues that
could involve several questions. There therefore is a need to introduce intermediate states, denoted by capitals, which correspond to a
set of questions, as a goal, being evaluated in a particular way. This
gives rise to a goal-driven structure.

A consultation may be considered to consist of the conjunction:

ZA1 AND ZA2 AND ZA3 AND ZA4 where:

ZA1	IF	(q44za1a = Y)
	OR	((q44za1a = ~Y) AND ZA1B)
ZA1B	IF	ZA1B1
	OR	(q44za1b2 = A)
ZA1B1	IF	(q44za1b1a = Y)
	OR	(q44za1b1b = Y)
ZA2	IF	(q44za1a = ~Y)
	OR	((q44za2a = Y) AND (q44za2b = Y))
	OR	ZA2C

ZA2C	IF	(q44za2c1 = Y)
	OR	ZA2C2
	OR	ZA2C3
	OR	(q44za2c4 = A)
ZA2C2	IF	((q44za2c2a = Y)
	AND	(q44za2c2b = Y))
ZA2C3	IF	((q44za2c3a = Y)
	AND	(q44za2c3b = Y))
ZA3	IF	(q44za1a = ~Y)
	OR	((q44za3a = Y)
	OR	(q44za3b = A))
ZA4	IF	(q44za1a = ~Y)
	OR	(q44za4 = A)

It should also be noted that there is identity between the following pairs:

    q44za2c1 = q44za3a
    q44za2c2a = q44za4

An alternative, and to some easier, way of describing these constraints is through the following diagram. In the Figure E.1 the nodes are questions, the answers (Y or ~Y) to which determine (via the arrows) the next questions to be asked.

E.5 Question Evaluation

This aspect of the expertise determines the assessment of the quality of the controls considered and what a relevant report should contain.

(a) The general case: Evaluation

Here I have taken an arbitrary measure of the overall quality of the software access controls. No expertise is represented in this section.

    Controls are good if tally > 29
    Controls are poor if tally < 21
    Otherwise controls are adequate.

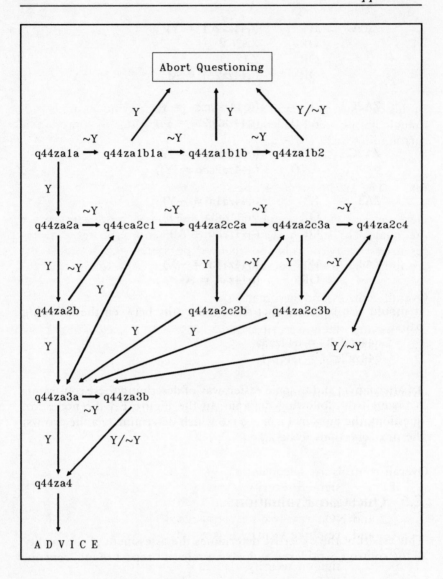

Figure E.1 Question asking constraints.

Tally is calculated by adding up the individual tallies for the questions: q44aiB, q44aii1B, q44aii2B, q44aii3B, q44aii4B, q44bi, q44bii, q44biii, q44biv, q44c, q44di, q44dii, q44e, where the individual tallies are allotted according to the state of the answers to the questions, thus:

Answer	*Tally*
Y	3
N	0
U	1

In this case only an overall assessment is produced, the output being a single phrase 'good', 'adequate', or 'poor' embedded in appropriate surrounding text.

(b)   The IBM System 34 case: Evaluation

Here the overall assessment is defined in terms of rules concerning the quality of sign-on security controls, menu security controls, resource security controls, and whether application specific passwords are used. The overall assessment is here referred to as 'overall'.

Overall controls are very good
    if   sign-on security is used
        and   menu security is used
        and   resource security is used
        and   application passwords are used as well

Overall controls are good
    if   sign-on security is used
        and   menu security is used
        and   resource security is used

Overall controls are adequate
    if   sign-on security is used
        and   menu security is used
        and NOT resource security is used
        and   resource security is covered
    or
            sign-on security is used
        and NOT menu security is used
        and   menu security is covered
        and   resource security is used

Overall controls are barely adequate
    if   sign-on security is used
        and   menu security is used
        and NOT resource security is used
        and NOT resource security is covered

    or
            sign-on security is used
        and NOT menu security is used
        and NOT menu security is covered
        and resource security is used
    or
            sign-on security is used
        and NOT menu security is used
        and menu security is covered
        and NOT resource security is used
        and resource security is covered

Overall controls are indeterminate
    if   any of {q44za1a, q44za2a, q44za2b, q44za3a, q44za3b,
            q44za2c1, q44za2c2a, q44za2c2b, q44za2c3a, q44za2c3b}
            is UNKNOWN

... otherwise ...

Overall controls are poor.

sign-on security is used
    if   (q44za1a = Y)

menu security is used
    if   (q44za2a = Y)
    and (q44za2b = Y)

resource security is used
    if   (q44za2c1 = Y)
    or   (q44za3a = Y)

menu security is covered
    if   resource security is used
    or   applications passwords are used in earnest

resource security is covered
    if   applications passwords are used in earnest
    or   (q44za3b = Y)

applications passwords are used in earnest
    if   (q44za2c2a = Y)
    and (q44za2c2b = Y)

application passwords are used as well
    if   (q44za4 = Y)

An overall assessment of a single embedded phase is generated
according to the above scheme. Thus software access controls can
be 'very good', 'good', 'adequate', 'barely adequate', 'poor' or 'indeterminate'. This is followed by a brief statement of the status of the
sign-on, menu and resource security controls.

A detailed assessment report is generated according to the
detailed values of the answers. However, each report is preceded by
an introduction and a summary of what might be considered as 'best
practice'. The text which is generated is therefore sometimes conditional upon answer values and sometimes not.

Condition(s)   *Text*

none   *Detailed Assessment*
               To ensure the continued smooth running of computer operations and the production of accurate information it is essential that the integrity of both programs and data files is maintained. This requires adequate controls to ensure the prevention of unauthorised updates to either live data or programs.

               The System 34 provides two types of security: sign-on security and file/library (resource) security. The former governs user access to the system and may include restrictions to particular program menus (menu security). The latter can be used to restrict access to designated files and program libraries. In addition, individual applications may have their own passwords associated with them.

               The use of sign-on security is absolutely essential in any installation. The absence of this fundamental control virtually precludes attempts to introduce other compensatory controls.

               Sign-on security permits the use of mandatory menus (menu security) so that users may be constrained in which system software they can access by virtue of their security profile which is determined by the attributes assigned to their user identification by the appropriate authority in their organisation.

In addition to access control via mandatory menus a user may also be constrained access by controls placed on the software itself. Thus a particular package may be accessed by particular users, this access being determined at the software rather than at the user.

In addition to access control via mandatory menus a user may also be constrained access by controls placed on the software itself. Thus a particular package may be accessed by particular users, this access being determined at the software rather than at the user.

Finally, individual programs may have passwords associated with them designed to control those who might wish to execute them.

q44za1a = ~Y
or
q44za2a = ~Y
or
q44za3a = ~Y   We believe that there are some deficiencies in the relevant procedures currently in force. Each of these is discussed in the ensuing paragraphs.

q44za1a = Y
and
q44za2a = Y
and
q44za3a = Y   In our opinion, the level of controls currently practised at the client's site would appear to be good. It would therefore seem unlikely that they would give rise to any significant business risk.

<sign-on security problems introduction>

Sign-on security

With regard to IBM System 34 sign-on security, each user must be assigned to one of four classes. A user is allowed to operate at any of the levels below his/her own class. The various classes of user are listed below in descending order of the level of access permitted:

(i) master security officer — effectively has unlimited access to the system and can run all system security utility programs;

(ii) security officer — allowed many of the privileges available to the master security officer but there are restrictions on which security programs they can run. However, security officers can both change their own passwords and set up and amend the security profiles of users assigned to one of the lower classes;

(iii) system operator — can use any terminal including the system console in sub-console mode, but cannot run any of the security utility programs.

(iv) display station operator — can use any display stations except those designated as system consoles or sub-consoles. They have no access to security programs.

q44za1a = N   <sign-on security problems introduction>
Our understanding is that sign-on security is not used at all. This means that there is virtually a total lack of IBM System 34 software access controls for the system and that consequently there may be severe risks involved.

q44za1b1a = Y   However, since the client has stated that he is using his own access control package, the actual degree of software access control in operation cannot be determined by IBM System 34 knowledge. The user is therefore advised that this expert system is of little use to him.

q44za1b1b = Y   However, since the client has stated that he is using a third-party access control package, the actual degree of software access control in operation cannot be determined by IBM System 34 knowledge. The user is therefore advised that this expert system is of little use to him.

q44za1b2 = Y   Although it is reported that physical access to terminals is restricted, it would be unwise to rely upon this as compensation for proper software access controls.

q44za1a = U   <sign-on security problems introduction>
Since it is not known if sign-on security is used at the client's site the reviewer should endeavour to

find out and, in particular, should ask for a report
of system security by users' IDs. This listing will
show the users IDs and their passwords plus their
class security officer, master security officer, etc.,
the service aids available to the user (this will
indicate whether a user has access to utilities such
as the dump and patch facilities that allow the
direct alteration of a file with no trace), the users
default library menu (i.e. indicating the menu with
which the user is presented when he signs on), and
whether the menu he is presented with is mandatory.

q44za1a = ~A   <sign-on security problems introduction>
At the moment I have insufficient information
about the client's sign-on security arrangements to
be able to make any comment.

<menu security problems introduction>
Menu security
Having defined the system users, the master security officer or a security officer can further restrict
users by assigning them to a specific menu. When
a user signs on, the authorised menu will automatically appear. This function is mediated by the
security profile (SECPROF) file. The security profile
is essential to any system of internal control and
should be thoroughly evaluated. If it is operating
successfully, it will ensure that users are only able
to access their own menus, thus enforcing segregation of duties and limiting the chance of unauthorised data accesses. As a result the only ones with
access to the system at large should be the master
security officer, the security officers, the system
operator and anyone not assigned to a menu.

q44za2a = N
or
q44za2b = N   <menu security problems introduction>

q44za2c1 = Y   It is our understanding that menu security is not
used but that the use of resource security is probab-
ly sufficient to compensate for this. Although
resource security measures alone may provide

reasonably secure access controls, there should be good reason for menu security not to be used for its continued non-use to be justified.

q44za2c1 = N   It is our understanding that menu security is not used and that resource security is not used to compensate for this. This situation could give great cause for concern.

q44za2c1 = U   It is our understanding that menu security is not used and that it is not known whether resource security is used to compensate for this. The reviewer ought to take measures to find out to what degree resource security is used to compensate for a lack of menu security.

q44za2c2a = Y
and
q44za2c2b = Y   However, it has been stated that access to individual applications is restricted by the use of application-specific passwords and that these passwords are capable of enforcing an appropriate segregation of duties. Relying purely on passwords for software access control must be considered hazardous unless the organisation is very small and informal. It is generally recommended that proper menu and resource security controls be implemented to minimise access control risk.

q44za2c2a = ~Y
and
q44za2c2b = ~Y   Also, it seems that there is no attempt to use application-specific passwords to compensate for the above which deepens the risk.

q44za2c3a = Y
and
q44za2c3b = Y   The client maintains that access to applications is controlled by non-IBM System 34 access control software and that this is also appropriate to enforce a segregation of duties. The reviewer is therefore advised that he should ensure that this is indeed the case and also that he should establish why

menu and resource security facilities are not being utilised at the site.

q44za2c4 = Y   In the absence of all software access controls with the exception of sign-on security, the client asserts that terminals are so located that the users are subject to continual supervision so disencouraging any unauthorised use of the computer system. This is really inadequate compensation for a lack of menu and resource security although it might carry more weight in a small and informal environment.

q44za2a = U
or
q44za2b = U   <menu security problems introduction>
                    Since it is not known if menu security is used at the client's installation the reviewer should endeavour to find out and in particular should review a listing of the SECPROF file obtained from the MSO. This review should ensure that users have been properly assigned to menus, programmers and security officers clearly defined, and the MSO status assigned to the DPM. Where the security profile is not appropriate for a specific user, immediate corrective audit recommendations should be made.

q44za1a = Y
and
q44za2a = ~A
or
q44za2b = ~A   I have insufficient information about the client's menu security arrangements to be able to make any comment.

<resource security problems introduction>
                    Resource security
                    Using file and library security (resource security) it is possible to protect particular files and/or program libraries by restricting access to them to designated users only. Four categories of authority may be given to a user:
                            (i) Execute: user may run programs from the protected library.

(ii) Read: user has execute authority and may also display the contents of the file or library.

(iii) Change: user has read authority and may also create, delete or amend the contents of the protected file or library.

(iv) Owner: user has change level access and may also grant access to other users or rename the file/library.

q44za3a = N   <resource security problems introduction>

q44za2a = N   The client has indicated that resource security is not used to protect access to sensitive program libraries and data files and in so doing may be incurring a serious risk especially since menu security is not being used.

q44za2a = Y   The client has indicated that resource security is not used to protect access to sensitive program libraries and data files and in so doing may be incurring a serious risk even though menu security is being used.

q44za2a = U   The client has indicated that resource security is not used to protect access to sensitive program libraries and data files and in so doing may be incurring serious risk.

q44za3b = Y   The client has also asserted that there are compensating procedures to protect sensitive program files and libraries. The reviewer should inspect these procedures and discover to what degree they are effective.

q44za3a = U   <resource security problems introduction>
In order to establish the usage of resource security by the client the reviewer should obtain and review a listing of the SECRES file and should perform the following steps:
• Compare the VTOC listing to the SECRES file listings to determine if all sensitive files are protected (the VTOC listing is a list of all files and libraries maintained by the system). For example, no master file should be unprotected. Before

reviewing SECRES, the reviewer should obtain a complete list of all master files.

• The various user categories should conform to predetermined information regarding who should be the owner, who is entitled to change or read the files, and who can execute programs. From this review the reviewer should ensure that programmers do not have access to live data files and production programs. Programmers should be restricted to only those files that they need in order to perform their functions.

q44za1a = Y
and
q44za3a = ~A   <resource security problems introduction>
                  Currently I have insufficient information about the client's resource security arrangements to be able to make any comment.

E.6 The Glossary

Basically the glossary consists of paragraphs of information about selected topics that it is anticipated the user might wish to consult. The user should be able to have access to this information at all times and at least while answering questions.

Sign-on security
Each user on an IBM System 34 computer has a user profile that consists of a user identification, his password, details of his badge (if any), special authorities (needed to perform operating functions), an initial program to be called when he signs on, and details of files and programs authorised for use.

A person who starts to use the IBM System 34 will be prompted for an identification and then for his badge (if badges are in use) and finally for a password. Thus at its simplest the password/badge security provide the overall access controls. They are important because they allow the unique identification of a user and therefore the definition of access rights that are appropriate to that particular user (determined by the client according to a user's responsibilities within the organisation) − in IBM terminology a {security profile}. This simple procedure to log on to the computer provides the basis of controls that are vital from the audit standpoint.

If a company does not have good control procedures designed to ensure the continuing confidentiality of passwords, and controls to ensure that profiles remain appropriate to users current functions the effectiveness of much of the other software access control procedures will be undermined.

Menu security

Menu security is the most often used method of controlling user access at clients. The nature of this method of control is simple and so it is easily understood by users. Therefore menu security is often the only security over and above the simple fact that a user needs to know a password to gain access at all.

Menu security allows each user to have a menu, customised to their specific functions and/or responsibilities. These menus can be mandatory or optional. In the case of optional menus the systems provide little security over and above the standard all or nothing approach discussed above. However, where mandatory menus are enforced, employees may only use the options available the menu specified for their use.

An enlightened site will determine menus that are appropriate to each function within their organisation and allocate the menus according to the user's task. At this sort of installation one would expect to see menus that are separate for each of the main ledger functions (nominal, purchases, sales, cash, etc.). Within each ledger function one expects to see normal menus available for the humble clerk and menus with greater privilege, that allow the update of masterfile details and permit the input of sensitive transactions, for use by the section supervisor or the accounts manager (depending upon the size of the organisation).

In practice menu security can give rise to some concerns where errors may exist in the software. One must take particular care that in the event of an error the software will not allow the user out of the original restricted menus. Software with errors will often return the user to the operating system which will undermine the security access controls provided by menu security and in these cases one is heavily dependent upon resource security.

Having defined the system users, the MSO or SO can further restrict users by assigning them to a specific menu. When a user signs on, the authorised menu will automatically appear.

The security profile (see SECPROF) is essential to any system of internal control and should be thoroughly evaluated. If it is operating well, it will ensure that users are only able to access their own menus, thus enforcing segregation of duties and limiting the chance of unauthorised data accesses. As a result, the only ones with access to the system at large are the MSO, SOs the OPS, and anyone not assigned to a menu, e.g. programmers. In some systems the operator is also assigned to a menu, thereby restricting his activities to only those functions needed to perform his duties. An audit comment might recommend that the operator be restricted to a menu in order to reduce the number of possible unauthorised accesses.

Resource security: Files and libraries

Resource security is designed to protect files, libraries, and peripherals. A file might be a collection of data relating to sales ledger masterfile information. A library is typically a file, containing program source code, job control procedures, executable program code, program subroutines or module program source code, job control procedures, and directories of these components.

The resource security is defined in terms of access rights, either by user IDs (specific access) and/or the access of all users (called public access). The rights granted can also be divided into a number of types of access: owner, change, read, and execute.

Resource security is mediated via the SECRES file.

Resource security: Devices as resources

Resource security allows each device to be controlled in the same manner as a library or file. In this way it is possible for a user to be excluded from particular terminals. For example this can be of particular use where one wishes to restrict the operation of the payroll to a terminal designated for payroll purposes.

Resource security: Application

The fact that all programs and data files are essentially files (possibly controlled within libraries) means that resource security can be used to provide a sophisticated method of access controls. However the control afforded is heavily dependent upon the care exercised when setting up the manner in which files/libraries are stored.

Resource security will typically be used to provide separate areas for each of the main accounting functions (e.g. payroll, nominal ledger, sales ledger, purchase ledger) and these will be structured to ensure that live software and data are separate. In addition to the main accounting areas separate areas will also be established so that utilities, programming tools (such as the editor, SEU, and the compiler, typically RPG) and programs currently being maintained are kept in separate development areas. The aim is to provide resource security, based around the protection of groups of resources that reflect different operations of the company (sales/purchases) or different types of entity on the computer (data/programs).

In practice most clients do not take full advantage of the resource security facilities and it is common to see just a few libraries to which all members of staff have access. The clients tend to rely on menu security and make little use of resource security.

Owner access
'Owners' have complete access rights to files and can grant access rights to other users as well as renaming files or libraries.

Change access
'Change access' allows a user the privileges of both 'read' and 'execute' access and in addition allows a user to create/delete files, libraries and library members. Also, users with this level of access can change the contents of individual files and library members.

Read access
'Read access' allows a user both to execute a program and also display the contents of that file on his terminal or within his library.

Execute Access
'Execute access' allows a program to be run, although it cannot be deleted or changed by the user.

Master security officer (MSO)
This person can:
- define password and badge security
- add, delete or edit profiles of security officers, system operators, sub-console operators, and display station operators
- change his own password and badge ID
- act as a system operator, sub-console operator or display station operator
- save and store security files

Security officer (SO)
This person can:
- add, delete or edit profiles of system operators, sub-console operators, and display station operators
- change his own password and badge ID
- act as a system operator, sub-console operator, or display station operator

- NOT run the utility programs that are necessary to save and restore security files (if he were able to do so he would be able to use another computer to undermine the master security officers access control this raises an interesting control point that all programs that are to be assigned the level of security of the master security officer must be carefully controlled if security is not to be compromised).

System operator (OP)
This person can:
- use any display station including the system console
- operate normal backup and other utilities
- NOT run the security utilities

Display station operator (DSO)
This person (the typical user) can:
- operate any display station not defined as consoles or sub-consoles
- run any utility other than those relating to security
- NOT run the security utilities

SECPROF
System security on the System 34 has two essential elements:

- A security profile (SECPROF)
- A resource security (SECRES).

The SECPROF defines all users of the system and records their passwords and access levels. This information is contained in the SECPROF file which is created (optionally) by the master security officer {(MSO)} when the machine is configured and can only be accessed in full by the MSO. The MSO is normally the data processing manager (DPM), the key person of the DP shop.

SECRES
System security on the System 34 has two essential elements:

- A security profile (SECPROF)
- A resource security (SECRES).

The SECRES contains a record for each protected file and library, the user IDs of the authorised users of each file or library, and an access code that identifies user categories. Any on-line file can be protected using SECRES to ensure that it is only accessed by authorised users. There are four user categories: owner, change, read, and execute.

For data files, the owner category should be restricted to the MSO. He is the only one who should have complete access to the system. Because of his high level of knowledge about the system, he is unlikely to accidently erase or duplicate files. To attempt to restrict the MSO's access is counterproductive. He can circumvent any access control.

Users of specific files can be assigned change status or read status, depending on user needs. The execute status will need to be assigned during menu creation in order to identify which programs a particular user can execute.

Source entry utility (SEU)

This system programming aid enables the user to enter display format specifications and program source statements directly into the system and to amend, copy or delete program source code.

Glossary

Artificial Intelligence
The discipline which concerns itself with the construction of artifacts which may be said to exhibit intelligent behaviour.

Backward chaining
Backward chaining is the control strategy in which an expert system is 'goal-driven', i.e. in which the truth of an assertion (often referred to in this context as a 'goal') is considered as a function of its constituent assertions (sub-goals), and so on until the lowest level assertions are data asked of the user or read from a file.

Control strategy
A protocol used for the manipulation of symbols leading to the evaluation of a set of assertions.

Data-driven
See Forward chaining

Decision support system
A system designed to provide support to decision makers through the manipulation and presentation of data, information, and knowledge.

Expert system
A computer-based system in which representations of expertise are stored and which allows a user to access this expertise in a way similar to that in which he might consult a human expert, with a similar result.

Expert system shell

A software package consisting essentially of an inference engine and a user interface but with an 'empty' knowledge base (hence 'shell'). The user is invited to construct his own knowledge base using a knowledge representation language provided with the package, the result being run as an expert system.

Forward chaining

Forward chaining is the control strategy in which an expert system is 'data-driven', that is, in which known facts or data are inspected, this then permits certain assertions to be evaluated, which then permit higher-level assertions to be evaluated.

Frame

A knowledge representation structure which describes objects in terms of attributes which take values.

Goal Driven

See Backward chaining

Heuristic

A rule of thumb that may be said to express 'compiled' or 'distilled' knowledge which has evolved in its owners mind over a long period by dint of his direct experience of the world.

Inference engine

An inference engine is a software device that operates upon a knowledge base (which, for example, may be a repository of production rules) according to a particular control strategy (for example, backward or forward chaining) during the course of which operation, and in conjunction with user data input, conclusions about the domain represented in the knowledge base are derived.

Knowledge acquisition

The process of capturing expertise from whatever source (for example, books, manuals, experts), for incorporation (after undergoing representation) into a knowledge base.

Knowledge base

That part of an expert system which contains the representation of the expertise or knowledge used by the system.

Knowledge elicitation
The process of encouraging an expert to articulate his knowledge in a particular domain of expertise.

Knowledge representation
The activity concerned with expressing an expert's knowledge in some symbolic form often using software as the medium.

Modus ponens
An argument of the following form is said to be in *modus ponens*:

> The truth of A implies the truth of B.
> A is true.
> Therefore B is true.

Production rule
A production rule is a that which is an expression of the *modus ponens* form of inference.

Prototype
An experimental version of a system constructed to explore the potential functionality of the envisaged completed system.

Semantic net
A knowledge representation structure consisting of a network of nodes interconnected by arcs, the nodes representing entities and the arcs representing relationships between those entities.

Shell
See Expert system shell.

Symbol manipulation
A process in which abstract symbols, which may represent objects in a particular domain, are manipulated in accordance with a particular protocol or control strategy.

User interface
That part of an expert system which manages the exchanges that take place between the system and the user.

References

Alter, S. (1980) *Decision Support Systems*, Addison-Wesley.

Amer, T., Bailey Jr. A., and De P. (1986) *A Survey of Computer Information Systems Research*, Faculty of Accounting and MIS, Ohio State University, Columbus, Ohio.

APEX, Technical Overview of PLANPOWER (1986) in *Applied Expert Systems*, Five Cambridge Center, Cambridge, MA 02142.

Arnold, M.E., Gambling, T.E. and Rush, D.G. (1985) Expert systems: as expert as accountants? *Management Accounting*.

Ash, N. (1985) How cash value appraises capital projects. *The Accountant*.

Bachant, J. and McDermott, J. (1984) R1 revisited: Four years in the trenches. *AI Magazine*, Fall 1984.

Bailey, A., Duke, G., Gerlach, J., *et al* (1985) TICOM and the analysis of internal controls. *Accounting Review*, Vol. LX, No. 2.

Bailey, A., Hackenbrack, K., De, P., and Dillard, J. (1986) *Artificial Intelligence, Cognitive Science and Computational Modelling in Auditing Research: A Research Approach*, Faculty of Accounting and MIS, Ohio State University, Columbus, Ohio.

Bakos, J.Y. and Treacy, M.E. (1986) Information technology and corporate strategy: a research perspective. *MIS Quarterly*.

Barr, A., and Feigenbaum, E.A. (1981) *The Handbook of Artificial Intelligence, -* Vol. I, Addison-Wesley.

Barras R. and Swan J. (1984) *The Adoption and Impact of Information Technology in the U.K. Accounting Profession*, The Technical Change Centre.

Bernstein, A. (1985) Money experts. *Business Computer Systems*.

Biggs, S. and Selfridge, M. (1986) GC-X: A prototype expert system for the auditor's going-concern judgement. *Symposium on Expert Systems and Audit Judgment*, University of Southern California.

Blanning, R.W. (1984) Management applications of expert systems. *Information and Management*, Vol. 7.

Boden, M. (1977) *Artificial Intelligence and Natural Man*, Harvester Press.

Bobrow, D. and Hayes, P. (1985) Artificial intelligence – where are we? *Artificial Intelligence*, No. 25.

Bonczek, R.H., Holsapple, C.W. and Whinston, A.B. (1980), Future directions in developing decision support systems, *Decision Sciences* Vol. 11, No. 4.

Bramer, M. (1982) in D.Michie (ed) *Introductory Readings in Expert Systems*, Gordon and Breach.

Buchanan, B.G. and Shortliffe, E.H. (1984) *Rule Based Expert Systems. The Mycin Experiment of the Stanford Heuristic Programming Project*, Addison-Wesley.

Buchanan, B.G. (1986) Expert systems: Working systems and the research literature. *Expert Systems*, Vol. 3, No. 1.

Chandrasekaren, B. (1983) in W. Reitman (ed) *Artificial Intelligence Applications for Business*, Ablex.

Clarke, F. and Cooper, J. (1985) *The Chartered Accountant in the Information Technology Age*, Coopers & Lybrand and ICAEW.

Collier, P.A. (1984) *The Impact of Information Technology on the Management Accountant*, ICMA.

Connell, N. (1987) Expert Systems: A review of some recent accounting applications. *Accounting and Business Research*, Vol. 17, No. 67.

Connell, N. (1987a) How successful are successful expert systems? *Operational Research Society Conference on Successful Applications of Expert Systems*, York.

Connell, N. (1987b) Development of a corporate strategy for the selection of appropriate application domains for expert systems. *End of Award Report: ERC Research Project No. F2425 0020.*

Connell, N. and Powell, P. (1987) *Success and Failure in the Commercial Application of Expert Systems*. Operational Research Society Conference, Edinburgh.

Connell, N. (1988) The current impact of expert systems on the accounting profession and some reasons for hesitancy in the adoption of such systems. *Knowledge Engineering Review*, Vol. 2, No. 3.

Cunningham, J. (1986), private correspondence.

d'Agapayeff, A. (1984) *Report of the Alvey Directorate on a Short Survey of Expert Systems in UK Business*, Alvey Directorate.

d'Agapayeff, A. (1986) A DP management update on expert systems. *Proceedings of the London Expert Systems Conference*, Mackintosh International.

d'Agapayeff, A. and Hawkins, C.B.J. (1987) *Report to the Alvey Directorate on the Second Short Survey of Expert Systems in UK Business*, Alvey News Supplement.

Davis, R. and Lenat, D.B. (1982) *Knowledge Based Systems in Artificial Intelligence*, McGraw-Hill.

Davis, R. (1982) Expert systems: where are we and where do we go from here? *AI Magazine.*

Dillard, J., and Mutchler, J. (1986) Knowledge-based expert computer systems for audit opinion decisions. *Symposium on Expert Systems and Audit Judgment*, University of Southern California.

Dreyfus, H.L. and Dreyfus, S.E. (1986) Why expert systems do not exhibit expertise. *IEEE Expert.*

Duda, R.O., and Gaschnig, J.G. (1981) Knowledge-based expert systems come of age. *Byte*.

Dungan, C.W. (1983) *A Model of an Audit Judgment in the Form of an Expert System*, PhD Dissertation, Department of Accounting, University of Illinois at Urbana.

Dungan, C.W. and Chandler, J.S. (1985) AUDITOR: A microcomputer based expert system to support auditors in the field. *Expert Systems*, Vol. 2, No. 4.

Edwards, A.V.J. (1986) What makes an expert? *Accountancy*, Vol. 98, No. 1119.

Edwards, A.V.J. (1987a) Mining for knowledge. *Accountancy*, Vol. 99, No. 1124.

Edwards, A.V.J. (1987b) What is the answer? In that case, what is the question? *Accountancy*, Vol. 100, No. 1128.

Ericsson, K.A., Simon, H. (1984) *Protocol Analysis: Verbal Reports as Data*, MIT Press.

Evens, M. (1986) Expert systems in the accountancy profession. *Proceedings of the London Expert Systems Conference*, Mackintosh International.

Expert Systems (1985) Financial Expert Systems from Apex. *Expert Systems*, Vol. 2, No. 4.

Feigenbaum, E.A., Buchanan, B.G. and Lederberg, J. (1971) On generality and problem solving: A case study using the DENDRAL program. *Machine Intelligence*, No. 6.

Feigenbaum, E.A. and McCorduck, P. (1983) *The Fifth Generation*, Michael Joseph.

Ford, F.N. (1985) Decision support systems and expert systems: A comparison. *Information and Management*, No. 8.

Friscia, A.J. (1985) AI market prospects are good. *The Industrial and Process Control Magazine*, March 1985.

Frost, R.A. (1985) Using semantic concepts to characterise various knowledge representation formalisms: A method of facilitating the interface of knowledge-base components. *Computer Journal*, Vol. 28, No. 2.

Frost and Sullivan (1986) *Artificial Intelligence Report*, New York.

Gambling, T. E. (1984) An expert system for governmental cost accounting standards. *Informal Discussion Paper*, Dept. of Business Studies, Portsmouth Polytechnic.

Goodall, A. (1985) *The Guide to Expert Systems*, Learned Information.

Gorry, G.A. and Scott-Morton, M.S. (1971) A framework for management information systems. *Sloan Management Review*, Vol. 13, No. 1.

Grindley, K. (1988) *The Price Waterhouse IT Review*, Price Waterhouse.

Grinyer, P.H. (1983) Financial modelling for planning in the U.K. *Long Range Planning*, Vol. 16, No. 5.

Grudnitski, G. (1986) A prototype of an internal control expert system for the sales/accounts receivable application. *Symposium on Expert Systems and Audit Judgment*, University of Southern California.

Hansen, J.V. and Messier, W.F. (1984) Continued development of a knowledge-based expert system for auditing advanced computer systems. *Preliminary Research Report, for Peat, Marwick, Mitchell*.

Hansen, J.V. and Messier, W.F. (1986) A preliminary investigation of EDP-XPERT. *Auditing: A Journal of Practice and Theory*, Vol. 6, No. 1.

Harmon, P. and King, D. (1985) *Expert Systems: Artificial Intelligence in Business*, John Wiley.

Hayes-Roth, F. (1984) in J. Fox (ed) *State of the Art Report*, Pergamon Infotech.

Hayes-Roth, F., Watermann, D. and Lenat, D. (eds) (1983) *Building Expert Systems*, Addison-Wesley.

Hellawell, R. (1980) A computer program for legal planning and analysis: taxation of stock redemptions. *Columbia Law Review*, Vol. 80, No. 7.

Hewett, J. and Sasson, R. (1986) *Expert Systems 1986: The Ovum Report*, Ovum.

Hogarth, R.M. (1987) *Judgement and Choice*, John Wiley.

Holroyd, P., Mallory, G., Price, D.H.R. *et al.* (1985) Developing expert systems for management applications. *Omega* Vol. 13, No. 1.

Holsapple, C.W., and Whinston, A.B. (1985) Management support through artificial intelligence. *Human Systems Management*, No. 5.

Johnson, P. (1986) Cognitive models of expertise. *Symposium on Expert Systems and Audit Judgment*, University of Southern California.

Johnson, P., Bailey, A., and Meservy, R. (1986) *Investigating Expertise in Auditing*. School of Management, University of Minnesota, Minneapolis.

Johnson, T. (1984) The commercial application of expert systems technology. *Knowledge Engineering Review*, Vol. 1, No. 1.

Keen, P.G.W. and Scott Morton M.S. (1978) *Decision Support Systems: An Organisational Perspective*, Addison-Wesley.

Kidd, A. (1985) in M. Merry (ed) *Expert Systems 85*, Cambridge University Press.

Klersey, G. and Mock, T. (1986) *Common Coding of Verbal Protocols in Accounting and Auditing*. Working Paper No. 93, Center for Accounting Research, School of Accounting, University of Southern California.

Lee, R.M. (1983) Expert vs. management support systems: semantic issues. *Cybernetics and Systems*, Vol. 14.

Macgregor J.M. (1982) *A Biased Survey of Corporate Modelling*, EPS Consultants.

Martins, G.R. (1984) The overselling of expert systems. *Datamation*.

McCarty, L.T. (1977) Reflections on TAXMAN: An experiment in artificial intelligence and legal reasoning. *Harvard Law Review*, Vol. 90, No. 5.

McDermott, J. (1981) R1, the formative years. *AI Magazine*, Summer 1981.

McDermott, J. (1982) R1: a rule-based configurer of computer systems. *Artificial Intelligence*, Vol. 19, No. 1.

McReynolds, B. (1984) Financial industries well suited for expert system applications. *SRI Journal*, Vol. 54, No. 4.

Meservy, R., Bailey, A. and Johnson, P. (1986) Internal control evaluation: A computational model of the review process. *Auditing: A Journal of Practice and Theory*, Vol. 6, No. 1.

Messier, W. and Hansen, J. (1984) in S. Moriarity and S. Joyce (eds) *Decision Making and Accounting: Current Research*, University of Oaklahoma.

Messier, W., Hansen, J. (1986) *Expert Systems in Auditing: The State of the Art*, University of Florida.

Michaelsen, R. and Michie, D. (1983) Expert systems in business. *Datamation*, November 1983.

Michaelsen, R. (1984) An expert system for federal tax planning. *Expert Systems*, Vol. 1, No. 2.

Milne, R. (1987) quoted in *Expert Systems 86*: Report on the Panel Session, in: British Computer Society Specialist Group on Expert Systems Newsletter No. 17.

Mintzberg, H. (1973) *The Nature of Managerial Work*, Harper and Row.

Newell, A. and Simon, H. (1972) *Human Problem Solving*, Prentice Hall.

Nii, H.P., Feigenbaum, E.A., Anton, J.J. *et al.* (1982) Signal-to-symbol transformation: HASP/SIAP a case study. *AI Magazine*.

Pasricha, N. and Evens, M. (1986) Building systems to do expert jobs. *Accountancy Age*.

Pattenden, N. (1986) quoted in *Expert Systems User*, June 1986.

Powell P. (1987) *The User as Modeller*, Department of Accounting and Management Science Working Paper, Southampton University.

Prerau, D.S. (1985) Selection of an appropriate domain for an expert system. *AI Magazine*, Vol. 6, No. 2.

Roycroft, A.E. and Loucopoulous, P. (1984) ACCI: An expert system for the apportionment of close companies' income. *Proceedings of Fourth Technical Conference of the British Computer Society Specialist Group on Expert Systems*, Cambridge University Press.

Schlobohm, D. (1985) Tax Advisor: a PROLOG program analyzing income tax issues. *Dr. Dobbs Journal*.

Schwartz, S.P. (ed) (1977) *Naming, Necessity and Natural Kinds*, Cornell University press.

Sell, P. (1986) *Management Strategy for Implementing Expert Systems*. Paper presented to a joint meeting of the Alfex and Aries Clubs.

Sen, A. and Biswas, G. (1985) Decision support systems: An expert systems approach. *Decision Support Systems*, No. 1.

Shafer, G. and Srivastava, R. (1986) *Managing Uncertainty in Expert Systems: A Perspective for Auditing*, Working Paper No. 182, School of Business, University of Kansas.

Shortliffe, E.H. (1976) *Computer-Based Medical Consultations: MYCIN*, Elsevier.

Shpilberg, D. and Graham, L. (1986) Developing ExperTAP: an expert system for corporate tax accrual and planning. *Symposium on Expert Systems and Audit Judgment*, University of Southern California.

Shpilberg, D., Graham, L. and Schatz, G. H. (1986) in *Expert Systems*, Vol. 3, No. 3.

Silvermann, B. (ed) (1987) *Expert Systems for Business*, Addison-Wesley.

Simon, H.A. (1960) *The New Science of Management Deceisions*, Harper and Row.

Smart, G. and Langeland-Knudsen, J. (1986) *The CRI Directory of Expert Systems*, Learned Information, Oxford.

Smith, H. (1984) On the development of commercial expert systems. *AI Magazine*.

Steinbart, P.J. (1986) The construction of a rule-based expert system as a method for studying materiality judgements. *Accounting Review*.

Stefik, M., Aikins, J., Balzer, R. *et al.* (1982) *The Organization of Expert Systems: A Prescriptive Tutorial*, Report VLSI-82-1, Xerox Palo Alto Research Centres.

Stoner, G. (1985) Expert systems: jargon or challenge? *Accountancy*.

Susskind, R. and Tindall, C. (1988), *VATIA: Ernst & Whinney's VAT Expert System*, Ernst & Whinney Working Paper, London.

Sussman, G., Winograd, T. and Charniak, E. (1970) *Microplanner*, MIT.

Torsun, I.S. (1986) in *Proceedings of the Sixth Technical Conference of the British Computer Society Specialist Group on Expert Systems*, Cambridge University Press.

Turban, E. and Watkins, P. (1988) *Decision Support and Expert Systems*, Macmillan.

Van Melle, W. (1979), A domain independent production rule system for consultation programs. *Heuristic Programming Project*, Department of Computer Science, Stanford University.

Willingham, J.J., Kelly, K.P. and Ribar, G.S. (1986) in *Proceedings of the 1986 Touche Ross/University of Kansas Auditing Symposium*.

Index